<u>Praise Waits for Thee in Zion:</u> _Strength For Your Inner Man_ by Dr. Marlene Miles

Freshwater Press 2025

Freshwaterpress9@gmail.com

ISBN: 978-1-967860-55-5

Paperback Version

Table of Contents

Praise 6

How To Praise.. 8

Praise Is 13

Old Testament Praise Verses 52

Bless the Lord 57

Lift Up Jesus 64

Songs 1 67

Songs 2 70

Songs 3 74

Songs 4 78

Wisdom 82

The Prophets 83

New Testament 88

Glorify God 91

Magnify 100

Majesty.. 104

Beauty 108

Strength... 110

God's Power 113

Exalt Him... 117

Extol the Lord 125

Praise Lyrics ♩♩ 126

Dear Reader 134

Prayerbooks by this author 135

Other books by this author 137

PRAISE WAITS FOR THEE IN ZION

Freshwater

All Scripture references taken from the KJV of the Holy Bible, unless otherwise indicated.

Praise Waits for Thee in Zion by Dr. Marlene Miles

Freshwater Press 2025

Freshwaterpress9@gmail.com

ISBN:

eBook Version

Praise

Praise waiteth for thee, O God, in Sion: and unto thee
shall the vow be performed.

O thou that hearest prayer, unto thee shall all flesh come.
(Psalm 65:1-2)

There are so many ways to praise the Lord. In church when the pastor or worship leader says, Praise the Lord, the congregation answers, "Hallelujah." We know Hallel, or Hallelujah, as the highest praise. We give God the praise of our lips, but it can be so much more than that. Sometimes it is a handclap and that is what the pastor or worship leader is asking for. But when real praise flows from you, it comes from the heart of you, out of your being and your belly – like living waters. So, as the Holy Spirit brings to our memory what we have put in by spending time in prayer, with the Lord, and in the Word, we will see how our praise develops and grows.

The difference between praise and worship is not that a praise song is fast and a worship song is slow. No, it's not that; it is the words that are spoken and the heart of the speaker/prayer toward God.

For clarity, praise is speaking well of a person (God) to others. While worship is speaking well of a person (God) to that person, (God). This book will focus on praise and the praises of our mouth or of our words. Oftentimes God will put a word of praise in your mouth and you may stay there for a while, a day, weeks, or even months. Maybe it will become your go-to praise. Well, Amen. But when the pastor or worship leader says, Praise the Lord and the music is playing and you re instructed to give the Lord some praise, what do you do? What do you say?

Praise is prayers, most often set to music. It is a step up from Thanksgiving and it is on the path to Worship. Thanksgiving may be at the Gate, but Praise is in the Courts of the Lord, while we may think of Worship as we ascend, we enter into the Holy of Holies. Amen.

When you pray it is best to pray the Word of God, so why not also praise from the Bible? This book is all about that praise, so read it, absorb it, say it, speak it, pray it, sing it, just praise the Lord & Amen.

This book will guide you if you need or want guidance to deepen your praise language and your praise itself. It is by no means a comprehensive volume as God is infinite and ways to praise him are many, varied and only subject to the Spirit of God and the heart of the one who is praising.

As you enter into the gates and ascend into the Courts of the Lord, your heart and zeal for the Lord lets Him know that Praise is waiting for the Lord God in Zion.

How To Praise

Exalt – raise God up, lift His name higher than any other.
Bless – speak good of the Lord.
Glorify – magnify, show His greatness.
Thank – gratitude itself becomes praise.

Rejoice – delight in God's presence and actions.
Magnify – zoom in so others see God's greatness clearly.
Adore – deep love expressed.
Celebrate – marking God's goodness with joy.

Extol

Lift Up

Old Testament (Hebrew) Words

Hallel – to celebrate, boast joyfully about God. Root of *Hallelujah!* That joyful, "Hallelujah" kind of praise. "Praise the LORD! Praise, O servants of the LORD, praise the name of the LORD!" (Psalm 113:1)

Yadah – to throw up the hands in thanks and adoration. Physical rejoicing. So, the slang use of yada-yada-yada to describe something boring, trite, or mundane is quite inappropriate, especially for professed Christians. Hands lifted, thanksgiving poured upward. "I will give thanks to You, O Lord, among the peoples; I will sing praises to You among the nations." (Psalm 108:3)

Todah – thanksgiving, often before the breakthrough comes. Thanks given even before the answer is visible. "He who offers a sacrifice of thanksgiving honors Me…" (Psalm 50:23). Thanksgiving gets you through the Gates of the Lord, Praise is what you do in His Courts.

Barak – to kneel and bless God with reverence. - Kneeling praise, reverent blessing of God. "I will bless the LORD at all times; His praise shall continually be in my mouth." (Psalm 34:1)

Tehillah – singing praise; a song of adoration (the very word "Psalms" comes from this idea). Singing our adoration.
"You are holy, enthroned on the praises of Israel." (Psalm 22:3)

Zamar – to make music, play instruments, pluck strings for God. Praise through instruments and music. "Sing praises to the LORD with the lyre, with the lyre and the sound of melody." (Psalm 98:5)

Shabach – to shout praise loudly, triumphantly, with authority.   -Triumphant   shouting.

"One generation will praise Your works to another and declare Your mighty acts." (Psalm 145:4)

Ranan – to ring out with joy; a jubilant cry. Joy so loud it rings out. "Sing joyfully to the Lord, you righteous; it is fitting for the upright to praise Him." (Psalm 33:1)

Gil – to spin or leap for joy The kind of joy that leaps and twirls. "Let Israel rejoice in their Maker; let the people of Zion be glad in their King." (Psalm 149:2)

Kabod – to give God glory; ascribe weight and honor. **Glorify-** To give God the weight and honor due His name. "Ascribe to the LORD the glory due His name; worship the LORD in the splendor of holiness." Psalm 29:2

Hodah / Hode – splendor and majesty expressed back to God.

Asah Shem – to "make His name great."

Ruwm – to exalt, lift high.

New Testament (Greek) Words

Aineo– to praise with words; extol publicly.

Eulogeo – to speak well of God; bless. (Our "eulogy" traces back here.) **Bless** - Speaking well of God.

"Blessed be the God and Father of our Lord Jesus Christ, who has blessed us…" (Ephesians 1:3)

Doxazo – to glorify; reveal God's honor and character.

Glorify - Revealing God's goodness and majesty. "So whether you eat or drink, or whatever you do, do all to the glory of God." (1 Corinthians 10:31)

Homologeo – to confess, agree with God's greatness out loud.

Proskuneo – to bow down, kiss toward God in worship. **Worship** - Bowing heart and life before Him. "Come, let us worship and bow down; let us kneel before the LORD our Maker." (Psalm 95:6)

Charis – grace; sometimes translated in contexts of giving thanks.

Eucharisteo – to give thanks (root of "Eucharist"). **Give thanks** – Gratitude offered as worship. "Give thanks in all circumstances; for this is the will of God in Christ Jesus for you." (1 Thessalonians 5:18)

Humneo – to sing praises, hymns.

Ruwm / Exalt Lifting God's name high. "Exalt the LORD our God and worship at His holy mountain, for the LORD our God is holy." Psalm 99:9

Aineo -New Testament praise spoken out loud. "And suddenly there was with the angel a multitude of the heavenly host praising God…" (Luke 2:13)

Each of these methods of praise gives us a slightly different way to approach God. Together, they show how praise can involve the whole person: mind, heart, voice, body, memory, and hope.

Worship - assigning ultimate worth.

Praise Is

Praise is calling the Names of God. Just as in the natural, praise is paying attention, looking on, looking at, speaking to, simply calling the name. Praise is calling the names of God because His Names are His attributes. They are His character. The following is a long list, but it is not exhaustive. They are praiseworthy names of God and names that indicate His Glory and His attributes, mostly in English with some Hebrew or Greek names. Just speak/pray/say these names and they will come alive for you. The Lord will reveal Himself to you in the attributes of whatever Names you call Him.

Abba—equivalent to: Daddy

Abi - Eternal Father

Adonai - My LORD

Advocate

The Almighty

The Alpha and the Omega
The All Sufficient One

The *Amen*
The Ancient of Days
The Anointed One - Christ and Messiah

The Atoning Sacrifice for Our Sins

The Author and Finisher of Our Faith

The Author of Life

The Author of Peace

Bara' Meaning: "The Creator of Israel"

The Beginning and End

The Blessed and Only Sovereign

The Blessed Hope

The Branch of Righteousness

The Bread of God *John 6:33*

The Bread of Life

The Brightness of His Glory

The Bright Morning Star

A Buckler to All Those that Trust In Him

A Buckler to Them That Walk Uprightly

By Whom All Things Were Made, Both in Heaven
and On Earth

The Chief Apostle
The Chief Cornerstone

The Chosen of God

The Christ of God

Christ Jesus

Christ Our Passover

Christ the Lord

Christ the Power of God

Christ the Power of God, and the Wisdom of God

The Comforter

Consolation of Israel

A Consuming Fire

Counselor

Creator of the Ends of the Earth

Dayspring From On High

The Daystar -

The Desire of All Nations
The Destroying Stone

The Door -

The Door of the Sheep

El or `El
El Berith
El Elohe Yisrael

El-Elohe-Israel or Elelohe Israel

El 'Elyon
El Gibhor – "The Mighty God"

Elohim

El Olam: The Everlasting God or The Eternal God

Eloi (Elói): "He Is"

El Shaddai -"God Almighty"

Elyown - "The Most High God"

The Eternal God

The Eternal One

Everlasting Father

The Everlasting God

Everlasting King

The Express Image of His Person

faithful and True

The Faithful Witness

The Faithful and True Witness

Faithful Creator

The Faithful God

The Father

The Father Almighty

The Father of Glory

The Father of Lights

The Father of Mercies

Father of the Fatherless

The Fear of the Lord—

The Firstborn From the Dead

The Firstborn of All Creation

The Firstborn Among Many Brothers

The Foundation Stone

The Fountain of Living Waters

Fullness of the Godhead Bodily

Glorious LORD

Glory of their strength

Glory of thy people Israel

God

God Almighty

God and Father of all

God Full of Compassion

God Manifest in the Flesh

God my Rock

God of Abraham
God of Abraham, God of Isaac, and God of Jacob
The God of All Flesh

The God of All Grace, Who Called Us to
His Eternal Glory by Christ Jesus

God of Forgiveness

The God of Glory

The God of Heaven

God of Heaven and Earth

God of Israel

God of Jacob

God of the upright

God of Justice

the God of Knowledge

God of Love

The God of Love and Peace

God of Me

God of My Life

God of mercy

God of My Mercy

God of My Praise

God of My Righteousness

God of Sarah, God of Rebecca, God of Leah, God
of Rachel
God of the Covenant

God of Your Fathers

God of Our Salvation

God of Patience and Consolation

The God of Peace

God of the Armies of Israel

The God of the Living

God of the Whole Earth

God of Thy Fathers

God of Truth and Without Iniquity

The Only Wise God

God our Rock

God our Savior

The God Ready to Pardon

God That Cannot Lie

God, Who Comforts the Downcast

The God Who Works Wonders

The God Who Answers By Fire

God Who Judges on Earth

God, who made the world and everything in it

God, The Holy Trinity

God Who Accomplishes All Things for Me

God Who is Near, Not Far Off

God Who Shows Mercy

God the Father

God, the Father Almighty, Maker of Heaven and Earth, and of All Things Visible and Invisible

God the LORD

God Who Always Leads Us in Triumph in Christ

God Who Does Great and Unsearchable Things, Wonders Without Number

The God Who Gives Us the Victory Through Our Lord Jesus Christ

God, The Holy Trinity

The God Who Has Been My Shepherd Throughout My Life to This Day

God Who Has Not Turned Away My Prayer

The God Who Raises the Dead

The God Who Sees

The Godhead

God's Servant

God's Righteous Servant

The Good Shepherd

Ruler Over All the Nations

Gracious and Merciful God

The Glorious LORD

The Great and Dreadful God

Great and Awesome God

The Great God

The Great God and Our Savior Jesus Christ

The Great God That Formed All Things

Great High Priest

The Great King Above All Gods

Great King Over All the Earth

The Great Shepherd of the Sheep

The Great, the Mighty, and the Awesome God

The Great Physician

HaShem "The Name"

The Head of the Church

The Help of My Countenance

The Helper

Helper of the Fatherless

He in Whom Are Hidden All the Treasures of Wisdom and Knowledge

He in Whom I Trust

He Is

He Who Sits On the Throne

The One Who Sits Enthroned from of Old

The Builder Of All Things

He That Called You Into Fellowship With His Son, Jesus Christ Our Lord

He Who Daily Bears Our Burden

He Who Made Heaven and Earth

He Who Calls You

He That Cometh From Above

"He who comes from heaven

"He Who Comes From Heaven"

He That Cometh In the Name of the Lord

He That Comforteth You

He That Createth the Wind

He Who Declares to Man What Are His Thoughts

He That Doth Speak

He That Filleth All In All

He That Giveth Breath Unto the People

He That Giveth Strength and Power Unto His People

He That Has Called Us to Glory and Virtue

He That Has Mercy On Them

He That Has the Seven Spirits of God

He That Holds the Seven Stars in His Right Hand

He Who Gave Himself a Ransom for All

him That Is Able to Do Exceeding Abundantly Above All That We Ask or Think

He That Is Able to Keep You From Falling

Him That Is Able to Present You Faultless Before the Presence of His Glory With Exceeding Joy

Him Who Made the Heavens

he That Is Higher Than the Highest

He Who Is Holy

He That Is Mighty

Him Who Is Able to Establish You

He Who Is True

He That Judgeth Righteously

He That Keepeth Israel

He That Keepeth Thee
He That Keepeth Thy Soul

"He who guards your soul" — *"The*

He Who Lives, and Was Dead

He Who Lives Forever and Ever

He Who Loves Us

He who makes dawn into darkness

He who made the Pleiades and Orion

He who Made the Great Lights

He who provides you with the Spirit

He who opens and no one shuts, and shuts and no one opens

He Who Weighs the Hearts

He That Raised Up Jesus From the Dead

He Who Reveals Mysteries

He That Rideth Upon the Heavens Of Heavens

He Who Sanctifies

He Who Searches Hearts

He Who Is Coming

He That Shall Have Dominion

He Who Sits in the Heavens

He Who Sits Above the Circle Of the Earth

He Who Sits on the Throne

He Who Struck Down the Firstborn of Egypt

He Who Did Not Spare His Own Son

He Who Warns From Heaven

He Who Flashes Forth With Devastation Upon the Strong

Him Who Spread Out the Earth Above the Waters

He That Took Me Out of the Womb

He That Turneth the Shadow of Death Into the Morning

He That Washed Us From Our Sins

He Who Works Miracles Among You

The One Who Baptizes With the Holy Spirit

He Who Stirs Up the Sea

He Gives Life to the World

The One Who Has the Sharp Two-Edged Sword

The Head of Every Man

The Head of Christ

The Head of the Church

Healer

The Chief Cornerstone

The High and Lofty One Who Inhabits Eternity

The Most High God Their Redeemer

The Highest One

Him Who Divided the Red Sea in Two

Him Which Is, and Which Was, and Which Is to Come

Him Which Is Perfect in Knowledge

Him Who Led His People Through the Wilderness

He who searches hearts and minds

He Which Smote Great Kings

He Who Establishes Us With You in Christ

The One Who Has Been Designated By God As Judge of the Living and the Dead

He Who Alone Does Great Wonders

He Who Built the House

He Who Has Called You Out of Darkness Into His Marvelous Light

He Who Has Eyes Like a Flame of Fire

He Who Walks in the Midst of the Seven Golden Candlesticks

He Who Works All Things According to the Counsel of His Will

He Whom God Hath Sent

him to Whom We Must Give Account

He Who Comes in the Name of the Lord

Our High Priest (or Chief Priest)

High priest Over the House of God

High Priest Forever After the Order of Melchizedek

Him Who Ought To Be Feared

Him Who Is Able to Establish You

His Anointed

His Dear Son

His Son From Heaven

His Spirit That Dwells In You

His Indescribable Gift

The Holy

Holy God
The Holy One

The Holy One and the Just

The Holy One, Blessed Be He

Hakodosh

The Holy One In Our Midst

The Holy One of God

The Holy One of Israel

The Holy Ghost

The Holy Spirit of Promise

Hope of Israel

The Hope of Israel, his Savior in time of trouble

The Hope of Our Fathers

Horn of My Salvation

A fortress To Save Me

Husband of Israel

I Am
I Am that I Am
"I AM WHO I AM"

I Am a Father to Israel

I Am a Great King

I Am Alive for Evermore

I Am Alpha and Omega

I Am for You

I Am From Above

I Am God

I Am God Almighty

I Am Gracious

I Am He Who Comforts You

I Am He Who Speaks

I Am He that Lives and Was Dead

I Am He Who Searches Minds and Hearts

I Am Holy

I Am in the Midst of Israel

I Am Married Unto You [Israel]

I Am Gentle and Humble In Heart

I Am Merciful

I Am Not of This World

I Am the Almighty God

I Am the Bread of Life

I Am the Door

I Am the Door of the Sheep

I Am the God of Abraham, and the God of Isaac, and the God of Jacob

I Am the God of Your Fathers

I Am the Living Bread That Came Down From Heaven

I Am the LORD

I Am The LORD, and There Is No Other

I Am Yahweh Who Makes You Holy

I Am the LORD That Heals You

I Am the LORD, the God of All Flesh

I Am the LORD Your God

I Am the LORD Your God from the Land of Egypt

I Am the Lord Your God Who Leads You In the Way You Should Go

I Am the Lord Your God Who Teaches You To Profit

I Am the Lord Who Shows Lovingkindness, Justice, and Righteousness On Earth

I Am the Lord Who Sanctifies You

I Am the Resurrection and the Life

The Root and the Offspring of David

I Am the Vine

I Am Their Inheritance
I Am Your Very Great Reward

I Am Your Portion and Your Inheritance
I Am Your Salvation

I Am With You

I Am With You To Deliver You

I Am With You To Save You

I Am With You Always

I That Speak in Righteousness, Mighty to Save

The Image of the Invisible God

Immanuel
The Invisible God

Israel's Creator

Israel's King

Jah

Jealous
Jealous God

Jehovah M'Kaddesh or *Yahweh M'Kaddesh*

Jehovah `Elohiym
Jehovah Jireh
Jehovah M'kaddesh"

Jehovah Nissi

Jehovah Ra'ah
Jehovah Rohi
Jehovah Rapha
Jehovah Rophe
Jehovah Sabaoth
The Lord of Hosts

Jehovah Shalom
Jehovah Shammah
Jehovah Tsidkenu
Je-Hoshua (or Jehoshua or Joshua)
Jesus Christ

Jesus Christ our Lord

Jesus Christ our Savior

Jesus Christ the Righteous

Jesus of Nazareth

Jesus of Galilee

Jesus, the Mediator of the new Covenant
Jesus, Son of God Most High

Jesus, Which Delivered Us From the Wrath to Come

Joshua -Yehoshua -"YHWH saves" or

The Judge

Judge of All the Earth

Judge of the Living and the Dead

Just God and Savior

The Just One
Kadosh (or *Qadosh*)
El Kanna
Thy Keeper
Holder of the Keys of Death and Hades

Holder of the Key of David

The King

The King Eternal, Immortal, Invisible

The King Forever and Ever

King of All the Earth

The King of Glory

King of Heaven

King of Israel

King of Jacob
King of Kings

King of Kings and Lord Of Lords

King of Nations

King of Saints

King of the Jews

Kýrios or *Kurios* "Lord" or "Master"

The Lamb

The Lamb Slain from the Foundation of the World

"The Lamb Slain Before the Foundation of the World"

The Lamb That Was Slain

The Last Adam

The Life

The Light

The Light of Mankind

Light of Israel

Light of the Gentiles

Light of the Nations

Light of the World

Light to Lighten the Gentiles

"A Light of Revelation to the Gentiles"

Lion of the Tribe of Judah

The Living Bread Which Came Down From Heaven

The Living Father

The Living God

The Living Stone

Logos
The LORD

Lord and Christ

Lord and Savior Jesus Christ

The LORD God

The Holy Trinity

The LORD God of Abraham, Isaac, and Israel

The LORD God of gods
The LORD God of Israel

The LORD God of My Salvation

Lord, Holy and True

The LORD Most High

The LORD God of Our Fathers

LORD God of recompense

LORD God of the Hebrews

Lord God of the Holy Prophets

LORD God of Truth

Lord of All

The Lord of Glory

Lord of Heaven and Earth

The LORD of Hosts

"Lord of the Hosts"

Lord Jesus

The Lord Jesus Christ, the Son of God, begotten of the Father

Lord of Kings

The LORD of Lords

The Lord of the Harvest

Lord God of Your Fathers

The Lord God Omnipotent

Lord Yahweh Who Gathers the Banished of Israel

The LORD Is Present
The LORD Mighty In Battle

The LORD My Banner
The LORD My Strength
The LORD My Shepherd
The Lord of Peace

The Lord of the Sabbath (Sabaoth)
The LORD on High

The LORD of Our Righteousness
The LORD Strong And Mighty

The Lord that Sanctifies

The LORD That Heals

The LORD That Is Faithful

The LORD That Smiteth
The LORD God of Hosts

The LORD the Judge

The LORD Thy God

The LORD Thy God from the Land of Egypt

The LORD Thy God in the Midst of Thee

The LORD Thy Redeemer

The LORD Which Hallows You

The LORD Which Will Help You

The LORD Who Will Provide
The LORD Who Teaches You to Profit, Who Leads
You in the Way You Should Go

The LORD Your God Which Goes Before You

The Lord's Christ

The LORD Our Peace
The LORD Our God

The LORD our Lord

The LORD that Smiteth

The Lord, Which Art, and Wast, and Shalt Be

The LORD Who Created the Heavens

God Who Formed the Earth

Lord Yahweh of Hosts

The LORD Your Redeemer

Love

The Majesty in the Heavens

The Majesty On High

The Maker of All Things

Man of Sorrows, and Aquainted With Grief

Man of War

Master

Master of the World
The Mediator of a Better Covenant

The Mediator of the New Testament

Melek, Melek kabowd
Melek Yisrael
Merciful and Faithful High Priest

Merciful God

Messiah
The Messiah the Prince

The Mighty

The Mighty God

The Mighty Terrible One

The Mighty God of Jacob

The Mighty One of Jacob
The Mighty One of Israel

My Elect One

My Holy One

Minister of the Sanctuary, and of the
True Tabernacle

The Morning Star

The Most High

The Most High God
The Most High Over All the Earth

The Most Holy

Most Mighty
My Beloved

My Beloved Son

My Buckler

My Defense

My Defense and Refuge in the Day of My Trouble

My Deliverer

"The Deliverer will come from Zion" —My
Exceeding Joy

My Father's God

My firstborn, higher than the kings of the Earth

My Fortress

My Friend

My Glory

My God

My Goodness

My Healer

My Help

My Helper

My Hiding Place

My Hiding Place and My Shield

My High Tower

My Hope

My Refuge in the Day of Calamity

My Judge

My King

My Lamp

My Portion Forever

My Portion in the Land of the Living

My Praise

My Refuge
My Refuge in the Day of Distress

My Refuge and My Portion

My Rock

My Salvation

My Savior

My Servant

My Shepherd

My Shield

My Song

My Support

My Strength and Power

My Strength and Song

Rock of Habitation to Which I May Continually Come

My Strong Refuge

My Strong Rock

My Mighty Rock

My Trust From My Youth

The Name

The One True God

One LORD

One Mediator Between God and Men

Only Begotten Son of God

The Only Begotten of the Father

The Only Lord God

The Only One

The Only True God

The Only Wise God

The Only Wise God Our Savior

Our Captain

Our Dwelling Place

Our Father
Our Father, Our King
Our Father Which Art in Heaven

Our God and Savior Jesus Christ

Our Guide

Our Hope of Glory

Our Judge

Our Lawgiver

Our Life

Our Lord Jesus Christ

Our Peace

Our Redeemer

Our Savior Jesus Christ

The Overcomer

The Pearl of Great Price

A Place of Broad rivers and Streams

Portion of My Inheritance and of My Cup

Only Sovereign
Precious Cornerstone

A Very Present Help in Trouble

Preserver of Men

Priest Upon His Throne

The Prince

Prince and Savior

The Prince of Life

Prince of Peace
Prince of Princes

Prince of the Kings of the Earth

The Promise of the Father

The Prophet

The Propitiation for Our Sins

Qanna'
Rabbi (or Rabbī)

Redeemer

Redeemer of Israel

Redeeming Angel
Refuge
Refuge for the Oppressed

A Refuge from the Storm

Refuge in Times of Trouble

The Resurrection and The Life

Rewarder of Them That Diligently Seek Him

The Righteous Branch

Righteous God and Savior

The Righteous Judge

The Righteous LORD

The Righteous One

Rivers of Water in a Dry Place

The Rock

The Everlasting Rock
(or The Eternal Rock or The Rock of Ages)

The Rock Who Begot You

The Rock That Is Higher Than I

Rock of His Salvation
Rock of Ages
(or The Everlasting Rock or The Eternal Rock)

Rock of Israel
The Rock of My Refuge
(or The Rock of Your Refuge)

Rock of My Salvation

Rock of My Strength

Rock of Offense [to both the houses of Israel]
Rod Out of the Stem of Jesse

The Root of Jesse

The Root of David

The Root and the Offspring of David

Ruach Elohim
Only Ruler
Ruler in Israel

Ruler Over the Nations

Sabaoth

The Salvation of God

The Salvation of Israel

The Sanctifier

Sar Shalom

"Prince of Peace"—Isaiah 9:6

Saving Strength of His Anointed

The Savior

The Savior of All Men

The Savior of the World

The Second Man

The Seed of Abraham

The Seven Spirits of God

Shaddai (or *Shadday*)

Shadow From the Heat

The Shadow of a Great Rock in a Weary Land

A Shelter

"A Refuge"

The Shepherd
The Shepherd and Overseer of Our Souls

Shepherd of Israel
My Shield
Shiloh
Shield of Abraham
Shield of Thy Help

A Shield to Those Who Walk in Integrity

The Son of God

The Son

Son of David

The Son of Man

The Son of the Blessed

Son of the Father

Son of the Highest

Son Over His Own House

Sophia
The Spirit

Spirit of Christ
Spirit of Counsel and Might

The Spirit of Glory and of God

Spirit of God
The Spirit of Grace

The Spirit of His Son

The Spirit of Holiness

The Spirit of Knowledge and of the Fear of the LORD

The Spirit of Life

The Spirit of Mercy

The Spirit of the Living God

The Spirit of the LORD

Spirit of Truth

The Spirit of Wisdom and Understanding

The Spirit of Your Father

A Star Out of Jacob

The Stone

A Tried Stone

Stone of Israel
A Stone of Stumbling [to the unbeliever]

The Stone Which the Builders Disallowed

Strength

Strength of Israel

Strength of My Heart

Strength of My Salvation

A Strength to the Needy in His Distress

A Strength to the Poor

The Striker of Abominations

The Strong One
Strong LORD

A Strong Tower from the Enemy

The Stumblingstone
Sun and Shield

Sun of Righteousness

Sure Foundation

Sword of Thy Excellency

That Man Whom He (God the Father) Has Ordained

Theos
Thine Everlasting Light

Thou that Dwellest Between the Cherubim

Thou that Dwellest in the Heavens

Thou that Hearest Prayer

Thou that Inhabitest the Praises of Israel

Thou That Lifts Me Up From the Gates of Death

Thou That Savest by Thy Right Hand

Thou Whom My Soul Loves

The True God

The True Bread from Heaven

The True Light

Thy Creator

Thy Exceeding Great Reward

Thy God that Pleadeth the Cause of His People

Thy Holy Child Jesus

Thy Life, and the Length of Thy Days

Thy Maker

Thy Shade upon Thy Right Hand

Tower of Salvation

The Trinity
The Triune God

The True Vine

The Truth
The Uncorruptible God

The Unspeakable Gift of God

The Vine

The Vine-Grower

The Way, the Truth, and the Life

Who Calls Into Being that which Does Not Exist

Who Will Have All Men to Be Saved

Who Alone Works Wonders [miracles]

Who Also Maketh Intercession for Us

Who Answered Me in the Day of My Distress

Who Calleth Those Things Which Be Not As Though They Were

Who Comforts Us in All Our Tribulation

Who Commanded the Light to Shine Out of Darkness

Who Covers Himself with Light

Who Crowneth Thee With Loving-kindness and Tender Mercies

Who Daily Bears Our Burdens

Who Forgiveth All Thine Iniquities

Who Gave Himself for Our Sins

Who Gives Life to the Dead

He Who Gives Food to All Flesh

Who Gives Rain Upon the Earth

Who Gives Songs in the Night

Who Gives Us Richly All Things to Enjoy

Who has Abolished Death

Who Has Also Sealed Us

Who Has Ascended Up Into Heaven

Who Has Bound the Waters in a Garment

Who Has Called You Unto His Kingdom and Glory

Who Has Established All the Ends of the Earth

Who Has Gathered the Wind in His Fists

Who Has Given Me Counsel

Who Has Given the Earnest of the Spirit In Our Hearts

Who Has His Eyes Like Unto a Flame of Fire

Who Has Redeemed My Soul Out of All Adversity

Who Has Redeemed Us From Our Enemies

Who Has Saved Us and Called Us With a Holy Calling

Who Has Done Great Things

Who Has Set Thy Glory Above The Heavens

Who Heals All Thy Diseases

Who Humbleth Himself to Behold the Things That Are In Heaven and in the Earth

Who Is Above All, and Through All

Who Is Blessed For Ever

Who Is Over All

Who Is Rich In Mercy

Who Is Worthy To Be Praised

Who Keepest Covenant and Mercy

Who Laid the Foundations of the Earth, That It Should Not Be Removed For Ever

He Walks Upon the Wings of the Wind

Who Liveth for Ever and Ever

Who Loved Me and Gave Himself For Me

Who Sets Up the Clouds To Be His Chariot

Who Maketh His Angels Spirits; His Ministers a Flaming Fire

Who Only Does Wondrous Things

Who Only Hath Immortality

Who Quickens All Things

"Who Gives Life To All Things"

Who Quickens the Dead

Who Redeems Your Life from Destruction

Who Remembered Us In Our Low Estate

"Who Remembered Us In Our Lowly State"

Who Satisfieth Thy Mouth With Good Things

"Who Satisfies Your Mouth With Good Things"

Who Shall Establish You, and Keep You From Evil

Who Stretches Out The Heavens Like a Curtain

Who Takes Vengeance

Who Walketh Upon the Wings of the Wind

Who Was Delivered For Our Offenses

Who Was Faithful to Him That Appointed Him

Who Was Raised Again for Our Justification

Who Was With Me in the Way Which I Went

A Witness to Us

Wonderful

Wonderful Counselor

The Word

The Word of Life

The Word of God

Yah [YH] or *Jah*

Yahweh
Yahweh Elohe Tsebaoth
Yahweh Elohim

Yahweh Our Righteouness
Yeshua - Yeshua Christ

You Who Are Enthroned Above the Cherubim
Your Healer

Your Fear

Your Heavenly Father

Your King

Your Holy One

Your Salvation

Zur - means, *Rock*

Old Testament Praise Verses

I praise the Lord, my hand *shall be* in the neck of thine enemies. (Genesis 49:8)

Let my first fruits be holy to praise the LORD. (Leviticus 19:24)

Lord, You are my praise, and my God. (Deuteronomy 10:21)

I praise You Lord, you have done great and terrible things, which my eyes have seen. (Deuteronomy 10:21)

I give You praise and honor, O Lord, my God. (Deuteronomy 26:19)

Praise ye the LORD for the avenging of Israel. I praise You Lord, for avenging me mine enemies, in the Name of Jesus. (Judges 5:2)

Hear, O ye kings; give ear, O ye princes; I, *even* I, will sing unto the LORD; I will sing *praise* to the LORD God of Israel. (Judges 5:3)

I thank and praise the LORD God of Israel, the God of Abraham, Isaac, Jacob. My God. (1 Chronicles 16:4)

And say ye, Save us, O God of our salvation, and gather us together, and deliver us from the heathen, that we may give thanks to thy holy name, *and* glory in thy praise. (1 Chronicles 16:35)

I stand every morning to thank and praise the LORD, and likewise at evening. (see, 1 Chronicles 23:30)

I will praise you on the stringed instrument, to give thanks and to praise the LORD. (1 Chronicles 25:3)

Now therefore, our God, we thank You, and praise Your glorious name. (2 Chronicles 29:13)

Praise the Lord, because his mercy *endureth* for ever. (2 Chronicles 7:6)

I will stand to praise the LORD God of Israel with a loud voice on high, (2 Chronicles 20:19)

I sing praise to the LORD, I praise You, Lord in the beauty of holiness. (2 Chronicles 20:21)

I praise the Lord, for His mercy *endureth* for ever. (2 Chronicles 20:21)

As I sing and praise the Lord, let Him set ambushments against my enemies, and smite them, in the Name of Jesus. (2 Chronicles 20:22)

I sing praises with gladness, and they bow my head to worshipped. (2 Chronicles 29:30)

Lord, I bring offerings of peace and give thanks, and praise in the gates of the tents of the LORD. (2 Chronicles 31:2)

With trumpets and cymbals, I praise the LORD, as David praised. (Ezra 3:10)

I bless the Lord God for ever and ever: and blessed be His glorious name, which is exalted above all blessing and praise. (Nehemiah 9:5, 12:24, 12:46)

And when the people saw him, they praised their god: for they said, Our god hath delivered into our hands our enemy, and the destroyer of our country, which slew many of us.(Judges 16:24) Thank You Lord, even though I have seen affliction, I have not been turned over to death.

I will call on the LORD, *who* *is* worthy to be praised: so shall I be saved from mine enemies. (2 Samuel 22;4)

For great *is* the Lord, and greatly to be praised: he also is to be feared above all gods. (2 Chronicles 16:25)

Blessed be the Lord God of Israel for ever and ever. And all the people said, Amen, and praised the Lord. (1 Chronicles 16:36)

It came even to pass, as the trumpeters and singers *were* as one, to make one sound to be heard in praising and thanking the LORD; and when they lifted up *their* voice with the trumpets and cymbals and instruments of musick, and praised the Lord, *saying*, For *he is* good; for his mercy *endureth* for ever: that *then* the house was filled with a cloud, even the house of the Lord. (2 Chronicles 5:13)

And when all the children of Israel saw how the fire came down, and the glory of the LORD upon the house, they bowed themselves with their faces to the ground upon the pavement, and worshipped, and praised the Lord, saying, for *he is* good; for his mercy endureth for ever. (2 Chronicles 7:3)

And the priests waited on their offices: the Levites also with instruments of musick of the Lord, which David the king had made to praise the Lord, because his mercy *endureth* for ever, when David praised by their ministry; and the priests sounded trumpets before them, and all Israel stood. (2 Chronicles 7:6)

And the children of Israel that were present at Jerusalem kept the feast of unleavened bread seven days with great gladness: and the Levites and the priest praised the Lord day by day, *singing* with loud instruments unto the Lord, (2 Chronicles 30:21)

And they sang together by course in praising and giving thanks unto the LORD; because *he is* good, for his mercy *endureth* for ever toward Israel. And all the people shouted with a great shout, when they praised the LORD, because the foundation of the house of the LORD was laid. (Ezra 3:11)

Also I shook my lap, and said, So God shake out every man from his house, and from his labour, that performeth not this promise, even thus be he shaken out, and emptied. And all the congregation said, Amen, and praised the LORD. And the people did according to this promise. (Nehemiah 5:13)

And at the end of the days I Nebuchadnezzar lifted up mine eyes unto heaven, and mine understanding returned unto me, and I blessed the most High, and I praised and honoured him that liveth for ever, whose dominion *is* an everlasting dominion, and his kingdom *is* from generation to generation: (Daniel 4:34)

God in whose hand that my breath is in, in whom is all my ways, I glorify You, in the Name of Jesus. (compare, Daniel 5:23)

Bless the Lord

When thou hast eaten and art full, then thou
shalt bless the LORD thy
God for the good land which he hath given thee.
(Deuteronomy 8:10) I bless You Lord, Jehovah Jireh,
you are my provider, for giving me good ground and
supplying all my needs according to Your riches in
Glory.

… Now bless the LORD our God, the God of our fathers
and I bow down my head and worship the Lord. He is
King forever and ever. (1 Chronicles 29:20)

I stand to bless the Lord my God for ever and ever: and
blessed be the glorious name, which is exalted above all
blessing and praise. Amen. (Nehemiah 9:5)

I will bless the LORD, who hath given me counsel: my
reins also instruct me in the night seasons. (Psalm 16:7)

My foot standeth in an even place: in the congregations
will bless the Lord. (Psalm 26:12)

I will bless the Lord at all times; his praise *shall* continually *be* in my mouth. (Psalm 34:1)

Bless the LORD, O my soul: and all that is within me, *bless* his holy name. (Psalm 103:1)

Bless the LORD, O my soul, and forget not all his benefits. (Psalm 103:2)

Bless the LORD, ye his angels, that excel in strength, that do his commandments, hearkening unto the voice of His word. (Psalm 103:20)

Bless the LORD, all his works in all places of his dominion: bless the LORD, O my soul. (Psalm 103:22)

Bless the LORD, O my soul. O LORD my God, thou art very great; thou art clothed with honour and majesty. (Psalm 104:1)

But we will bless the LORD from this time forth and for evermore. Praise the LORD. (Psalm 115:18)

I lift up my hands in the sanctuary, and bless the Lord. (Psalm 134:2)

Bless the LORD, O house of Israel: bless the Lord, O house of Aaron: (Psalm 135:19)

Bless the LORD, O house of Levi: ye that fear the LORD, bless the LORD. (Psalm 135:20)

Father, You are the God of Abraham my father: I do not fear; You re with me and You will bless me, and multiply my seed for my servant Abraham's sake. Therefore I will bless the Lord. Amen. (Genesis 26:24)

I bless the Lord, He gives and blesses my bread and water, and He blesses me, Amen. (see, Exodus 23:25)

I bless the LORD and He blesses and keeps me. (Numbers 6:24)

I bless You Lord because in blessing You have blessed me, and in multiplying, You have multiplied me, in the Name of Jesus.

I bless the Lord for He has made me able to bless and be a blessing to others.

I bless the Lord for He blessed me in all the works of my hands. (Deuteronomy 14:29)

I bless the Lord for He has greatly blessed me in the land which He has given me for an inheritance and to possess it, in the Name of Jesus. (Deuteronomy 15:4)

I bless the LORD for you have surely blessed all my works and all that I have put my hands to do. (Deuteronomy 15:10, 18; 23:20; 24:19)

I bless You, LORD God for You have blessed me in all my increase, and in all the works of my hands, therefore thou shalt surely rejoice. I make my boast in You. (Deuteronomy 16:15)

And the priests the sons of Levi shall come near; for them the LORD thy God hath chosen to minister unto him, and to bless the name of the Lord. (Deuteronomy 21:5)

I bless the LORD, He has commanded the blessing upon me and upon my storehouses, and in all that I have set my hand unto; and he shall bless in the land which the Lord thy God giveth thee. (Deuteronomy 28:8)

I praise You Lord, for you have opened up Your good treasure The LORD shall open unto thee his good treasure, the heaven to give the rain unto thy land in his season, and to bless all the work of thine hand: and thou shalt lend unto many nations, and thou shalt not borrow. (Deuteronomy 28:12)

I love the Lord God, I thank Him, I bless Him. Lord, let me walk in Your ways, keep your commandments, statutes, and judgments, that I may live and multiply. Lord, bless me in the land where I go to possess it, in the Name of Jesus. (compare, Deuteronomy 30:16)

Bless, Lord, his substance, and accept the work of his hands: smite through the loins of them that rise against him, and of them that hate him, that they rise not again. (Deuteronomy 33:11)

Bless the Lord, let all nations, let everyone, bless His Holy Name. (compare Joshua 8:33)

His Government is pure; it is on the shoulders of Jesus, andit shall last forever. Bless ye the Lord. (compare Judges 5:9, Isaiah 61)

Therefore now let it please thee to bless the house of they servant, that it may continue forever before thee: for thou, O Lord God hast spoken it; and with they blessing let the house of thy servant be blessed for ever. (2 Samuel 7:29)

I bless the house of the LORD, it is a just House magnificent in strength and beauty; let it be blessed forever, Amen.

I bless the Lord God, King of kings. His Name is great and greatly to be praised. His throne endures into all generations, and even forever. Amen. (compare 1 Kings 1:47)

I bless the House of the Lord, for it is blessed, O Lord, and *it shall be* blessed for ever. (comp.1 Chronicles 17:27)

The sons of Amram; Aaron and Moses: and Aaron was separated that he should sanctify the most holy things, he and his sons for ever, to burn incense before the Lord to minister unto him, and to bless in his name for ever. (2 Chronicles 23:13)

For thou, Lord, wilt bless the righteous; with favour wilt thou compass him as *with* a shield. (Psalm 5:12)

The LORD will give strength unto his people; the Lord will bless his people with peace. (Psalm 29:11)

I will call upon the LORD, *who is worthy* to be praised: so shall I be saved from mine enemies. (Psalm 18:3)

Great *is* the   LORD, and greatly to   be praised in   the city of our God, *in* the mountain of his holiness. (Psalm 48:1)

Bless ye God in the congregations, *even* the Lord, from t he fountain of Israel. (Psalm 68:26)

Sing unto the LORD, bless his   name; shew   forth his salvation from day to day. (Psalm 96:2)

Bless ye the Lord, all ye his hosts; ye ministers of his, that do his pleasure. (Psalm 103:21)

Let the sinners be consumed out of the earth, and let the wicked be no more. Bless thou the Lord, O my soul. Praise ye the Lord. (Psalm 104:35)

I bless the Lord. He is mindful of us, he blesses us, he blesses the house of Israel, he blesses the house of Aaron. (compare Psalm 115:12)

I bless You Lord, for you bless them that fear the Lord, *both* small and great. (Psalm 115:13)

I bless the Lord. Let Zion bless the Lord. For the Lord shall bless thee out of Zion; and thou shalt see the good of Jerusalem all the days of thy life. (Psalm 128:5)

I bless the Lord, let the blessings of the Lord be upon the people. I bless you, we bless you in the Name of the Lord. (compare Psalm 129:8)

Behold, bless ye the LORD, all *ye* servants of the LORD , which by night stand in the house of the Lord. (Psalm 134:1)

I bless the LORD, the LORD that made heaven and earth, who blesses me out of Zion. (compare Psalm 134:3)

My mouth shall speak the praise of the Lord and let all flesh bless his holy name for ever and ever. (Psalm 145:21)

And one cried unto another, and said, Holy, holy, holy, *is* the LORD of hosts: the whole earth *is* full of his glory. (Isaiah 6:3)

And thou shalt swear, the Lord liveth, in truth, in judgment, and in righteousness; and the nations shall bless themselves in him, an in him shall they glory. (Jeremiah 4:2)

The Lord bless, thee, O habitation of justice, *and* mountain of holiness. (Jeremiah 31:23b)

Lift Up Jesus

♪♪ How to reach the masses, men of every birth,
(help me lift Him up).
For an answer, Jesus gave the key,
(help me lift Him up). (*Help Me Lift Him Up*, Keith Pringle)

Let us lift up our heart with *our* hands unto God in the heavens. (Lamentations 3:41) Let us lift up the Lord, Our God.

And as Moses lifted up the serpent in the wilderness, ev en so must the Son of man be lifted up: (John 3:14) Let us lift up the Lord, Jesus Christ.

Then said Jesus unto them, When ye have lifted up the Son of man, then shall ye know that I am he, and that I do nothing of myself; but as my Father hath taught me, I speak these things. (John 8:28)

And I, if I be lifted up from the earth, will draw all men unto me. (John 12:32)

The people answered him, We have heard out of the law that Christ abideth for ever: and how sayest thou, The son of man must be lifted up. Who is this Son of man? (John 12:34)

I praise the Lord; I lift Him on high.

And that bringeth me forth from mine enemies: thou also hast lifted me up on high above them that rose up against me: thou hast delivered me from the violent man. (2 Samuel 22:49)

I will extol thee, O Lord; for thou hast lifted me up, and hast not made my foes to rejoice over me. (Psalm 30:1)

And he came and took her by the hand, and lifted her up; and immediately the fever left her, and she ministered unto them. (Mark 1:31) I exalt You, Lord. I extol You, for when I was sick, you lifted me. I praise You for Your wonderful goodness to the children of men.

I lift up Jesus; He has lifted me. Amen. But Jesus took him by the hand, and lifted him up; and he arose. (Mark 9:27)

I praise You, Lord, You are my strength. And he took him by the right hand, and lifted him up: and immediately his feet and ankle bones received strength. (Acts 3:7)

Lord, You are the lifter of my head, the lifter of my spirit, soul and body. I lift You on High. Amen. And he gave her his hand, and lifted her up, and when he had called the saints and widows, presented her alive. (Acts 9:41)

Lift up thyself, thou judge of the earth: render a reward to the proud. (Psalm 94:2)

I will lift up mine eyes unto the hills, from whence cometh my help. (Psalm 121:1) The Lord is high and lifted up, seated on His Throne. (Isaiah 6:1) He is the Maker of Heaven and Earth.

Now will I rise, saith the LORD; now will I be exalted; now will I lift up myself. (Isaiah 33:10) Arise, Lord, to thy resting place.

Humble yourselves in the sight of the Lord, and he shall lift you up.(James 4:10)

You are the lifter of my head...

I praise the Lord, for it is He who has awakened me from sleep and has given me the Light of His Love, the Light of His Mercy, the Light of the Kingdom, His Grace and His Truth. (see, Ephesians 5:14)

We have also a more sure word of prophecy; whereunto ye do well that ye take heed, as unto a light that shineth in a dark place, until the day dawn, and the day star arise in your hearts. (2 Peter 1:19)

Daystar, arise; be ye lift up, be glorified and ever lift up, Amen.

Songs 1

The heavens declare the glory of God; and the firmament sheweth his handywork. (Psalm 19:1)

I will praise the LORD according to his righteousness: and will sing praise to the name of the LORD most high. (Psalm 7:17)

I will praise *thee*, O LORD, with my whole heart; I will shew forth all thy marvellous works. (Psalm 9:1)

I will be glad and rejoice in thee: I will sing praise to thy name, O thou most High. (Psalm 9:2)

I may show forth all thy praise in the gates of Zion: I will rejoice in thy salvation. (Psalm 9:14)

Be thou exalted, LORD, in thine own strength: *so* will we sing and praise thy power. (Psalm 21:13)

I will declare thy name unto my brethren: in the midst of the congregation will I praise thee. (Psalm 22:22)

Ye that fear the LORD, praise him; all ye the seed of Jacob, glorify him; and fear him, all ye the seed of Israel. (Psalm 22:23)

My praise *shall be* of thee in the great congregation: I will pay my vows before them that fear him. (Psalm 22:25)

The meek shall eat and be satisfied: they shall praise the LORD that seek him: your heart shall live for ever. (Psalm 22:26)

The LORD *is* my strength and my shield; my heart trusted in him, and I am helped: therefore my heart greatly rejoiceth; and with my song will I praise him. (Psalm 28:7)

I will praise You, O Lord, so the rocks and the dust shall not have to cry out. (see (Psalm 30:9)

Lord, let *my* glory may sing praise to thee, and not be silent. O LORD my God, I will give thanks unto thee for ever. (Psalm 30:12)

Rejoice in the LORD, O ye righteous: *for* praise is comely for the upright. (Psalm 33:1)

Praise the LORD with harp: sing unto him with the psaltery *and* an instrument of ten strings. (Psalm 33:2)

I will bless the Lord at all times; his praise *shall* continually *be* in my mouth. (Psalm 34:1)

I will give thee thanks in the great congregation: I will praise thee among much people. (Psalm 35:18)

And my tongue shall speak of thy righteousness *and* of thy praise all the day long. (Psalm 35:28)

And he hath put a new song in my mouth, *even* praise unto our God: many shall see *it*, and fear, and shall trust in the LORD. (Psalm 40:3)

When I remember these *things*, I pour out my soul in me: for I had gone with the multitude, I went with them to the house of God, with the voice of joy and praise, with a multitude that kept holyday. (Psalm 42:4)

I shall praise God *for* the help of His countenance. (Psalm 42:5)

I will praise Him, shall yet praise him, *who is* the health of my countenance, and my God. (Psalm 42:11)

Then will I go unto the altar of God, unto God my exceeding joy. Upon the harp will I praise thee, O God my God. (Psalm 43:4,5)

In God we boast all the day long, and praise thy name for ever. Selah. (Psalm 44:8)

I will make thy name to be remembered in all generations: therefore shall the people praise thee for ever and ever. (Psalm 45:17)

According to thy name, O God, so *is* thy praise unto the ends of the earth: thy right hand is full of righteousness. (Psalm 48:10)

Lord, You bless my soul. Let *men* praise You, when thou doest well to thyself. (Psalm 49:18)

Songs 2

Lord, I glorify you by offering praise; show me Your salvation. (Psalm 50:23)

O Lord, open thou my lips; and my mouth shall shew forth thy praise. (Psalm 51:15)

I will praise thee for ever, because thou hast done *it*: and I will wait on thy name; for *it is* good before thy saints. (Psalm 52:9)

I will freely sacrifice unto thee: I will praise thy name, O LORD; for *it is* good. (Psalm 54:6)

In God I will praise his word, in God I have put my trust; I will not fear what flesh can do unto me. (Psalm 56:4)

In God will I praise *his* word: in the LORD will I praise *his* word. (Psalm 56:10)

My heart is fixed, O God, my heart is fixed: I will sing and give praise. (Psalm 57:7)

I will praise thee, O Lord, among the people: I will sing unto thee among the nations. (Psalm 57:9)

So will I sing praise unto thy name for ever, that I may daily perform my vows. (Psalm 61:8)

. Because thy lovingkindness *is* better than life, my lips shall praise thee. (Psalm 63:3)

My soul shall be satisfied as *with* marrow and fatness; and my mouth shall praise *thee* with joyful lips: (Psalm 63:5)

Praise waits for thee, O God, in Zion: (Psalm 65:1)

Sing forth the honour of his name: make his praise glorious. (Psalm 66:2)

O bless our God, ye people, and make the voice of his praise to be heard. (Psalm 66:8)

Let the people praise thee, O God; let all the people praise thee. (Psalm 67:3, 5)

I will praise the name of God with a song, and will magnify him with thanksgiving. (Psalm 69:30)

Let the heaven and earth praise him, the seas, and every thing that moveth therein. (Psalm 69:34)

Lord, You have kept me from my birth. You took me out of my mother's womb: my praise *shall be* continually of thee. (Psalm 71:6)

Let my mouth be filled *with* thy praise *and with* thy honour all the day. (Psalm 71:8)

But I will hope continually, and will yet praise thee more and more. (Psalm 71:14)

I will also praise thee with the psaltery, *even* thy truth, O my God: unto thee will I sing with the harp, O thou Holy One of Israel. (Psalm 71:22)

And he shall live, and to him shall be given of the gold of Sheba: prayer also shall be made for him continually; *and* daily shall he be praised. (Psalm 72:15)

O let not the oppressed return ashamed: let the poor and needy praise thy name. (Psalm 74:21)

Surely the wrath of man shall praise thee: the remainder of wrath shalt though restrain. (Psalm 76:10)

So we thy people and sheep of thy pasture will give thee thanks for ever: we will shew forth thy praise to all generations. (Psalm 79:13)

I will praise thee, O Lord my God, with all my heart: and I will glorify thy name for evermore. (Psalm 85:12)

And the heavens shall praise thy wonders, O LORD: thy faithfulness also in the congregation of the saints. (Psalm 89:5)

Lord, thou hast been our dwelling place in all generations.

Before the mountains were brought forth, or ever thou hadst formed the earth and the world, even from everlasting to everlasting, thou art God. Thou turnest man to destruction; and sayest, Return, ye children of men. (Psalm 90:1-3)

… LORD **God** of Abraham, Isaac, and of Israel, let it be known this day that thou art God in Israel, and that I *am* thy servant, and that I have done all these things at thy word. (1 Kings 18:36)

And now, Lord, thou art God, and hast promised this goodness unto thy servant:(1 Chronicles 17:26)

For thou *art* great and doest wondrous things: thou *art* God alone. (Psalm 86:10)

And when they heard that, they lifted up their voice to God with one accord, and said, Lord, thou *art* God which has made heaven, and earth, and the sea, and all that in them is: (Acts 4:24)

For the Lord *is* great, and greatly to be praised; he *is* to be feared above all gods. (Psalm 96:4)

Make a joyful noise unto the LORD, all the earth: make a loud noise, and rejoice, and sing praise. (Psalm 98:4)

Let them praise thy great and terrible name; *for* it *is* holy. (Psalm 99:3)

Songs 3

Make a joyful noise unto the LORD, all ye lands. (Psalm 100:1)

Enter into his gates with thanksgiving, *and* into his courts with praise: be thankful unto him, *and* bless his name. (Psalm 100:4)

This shall be written for the generation to come: and the people which shall be created shall praise the LORD. (Psalm 102:18)

I declare the name of the LORD in Zion, and his praise in Jerusalem. (Psalm 102:21)

I will sing unto the LORD as long as I live: I will sing praise to my God while I have my being. (Psalm 104:33)

Let the sinners be consumed out of the earth, and let the wicked be no more. (Psalm 104:35)

Bless thou the LORD, O my soul. Praise ye the LORD. (Psalm 104:35)

Praise ye the LORD. O give thanks unto the LORD; for *he is* good: for his mercy *endureth* for ever. (Psalm 106:1)

Who can utter the mighty acts of the LORD? *who* can shew forth all his praise? (Psalm 106:2)

Lord, I believe Your Words and I sing Your praise. (Psalm 106:12)

Save us, O LORD our God, and gather us from among the heathen, to give thanks unto thy holy name, *and* to triumph in thy praise. (Psalm 106:47)

Blessed *be* the Lord God of Israel from everlasting to everlasting and let all the people say, Amen. Praise ye the Lord. (Psalm 106:48)

Oh that *men* would praise the Lord *for* his goodness, and *for* his wonderful works to the children of men! (Psalm 107:8, 15, 21, 31)

Let them exalt him also in the congregation of the people, and praise him in the assembly of the elders. (Psalm 107:32)

O God, my heart is fixed; I will sing and give praise, even with my glory. (Psalm 108:1)

I will praise thee, O Lord, among the people: and I will sing praises unto thee among the nations. (Psalm 108:3)

Hold not thy peace, O God of my praise. (Psalm 109:1)

I will greatly praise the Lord with my mouth; yea, I will praise him among the multitude. (Psalm 109:30)

Praise ye the Lord, I will praise the Lord with *my* whole heart, in the assembly of the upright, and *in* the congregation. (Psalm 111:1)

The fear of the LORD *is* the beginning of wisdom: a good understanding have all they that do *his commandments*: his praise endureth for ever. (Psalm 111:10)

Praise ye the LORD. Blessed *is* the man *that* feareth the LORD, *that* delighteth greatly in his commandments. (Psalm 112:1)

Praise ye the LORD. Praise, O ye servants of the Lord, praise the name of the LORD. (Psalm 113:1)

From the rising of the sun unto the going down of the same the LORD'S name *is* to be praised. (Psalm 113:3)

He maketh the barren woman to keep house, *and to be* a joyful mother of children. Praise ye the LORD. (Psalm 113:9)

But we will bless the LORD from this time forth and for evermore. Praise the LORD. (Psalm 115:18)

In the courts of the LORD'S house, in the midst of thee, O Jerusalem. Praise ye the LORD. (Psalm 116:19)

O praise the LORD, all ye nations: praise him, all ye people. (Psalm 117:1)

For his merciful kindness is great toward us: and the truth of the LORD *endureth* for ever. Praise ye the LORD. (Psalm 117:2)

Open to me the gates of righteousness: I will go into them, *and* I will praise the LORD. (Psalm 118:19)

I will praise thee: for thou hast heard me, and art become my salvation. (Psalm 118:21)

Thou *art* my God, and I will praise thee: *thou art* my God, I will exalt thee. (Psalm 118:28)

I will praise thee with uprightness of heart, when I shall have learned thy righteous judgments. (Psalm 119:7)

The earth, O LORD, is full of thy mercy: teach me thy statutes. (Psalm 119:64)

Seven times a day do I praise thee because of thy righteous judgments. (Psalm 119:164)

My lips shall utter praise, when thou hast taught me thy statutes. (Psalm 119:171)

Let my soul live, and it shall praise thee; and let thy judgments help me. (Psalm 119:175)

Songs 4

Praise ye the Lord. Praise ye the name of the Lord; praise *him*. O ye servants of the Lord. (Psalm 135:1)

Praise the LORD, for the LORD; for the LORD is good: sing praises unto his name; for *it is* pleasant. (Psalm 135:3)

Blessed be the LORD out of Zion, which dwelleth at Jerusalem. Praise ye the LORD. (Psalm 135:21)

I will praise thee with my whole heart: before the gods will I sing praise unto thee. (Psalm 138:1)

I will worship toward thy holy temple, and praise thy name for thy lovingkindness and for thy truth: for thou hast magnified thy word above all thy name. (Psalm 138:2)

All the kings of the earth shall praise thee, O Lord, when they hear the words of thy mouth. (Psalm 138:4)

I will praise thee; for I am fearfully and wonderfully made; marvellous *are* thy works; and *that* my soul knoweth right well. (Psalm 139:14)

Bring my soul out of prison, that I may praise thy name: the righteous shall compass me about; for thou shalt deal bountifully with me. (Psalm 142:7)

I will extol thee, my God, O king; and I will bless thy name for ever and ever. (Psalm 145:1)

Every day will I bless thee; and I will praise thy name for ever and ever. (Psalm 145:2)

Great *is* the LORD, and greatly to be praised; and his greatness *is* unsearchable. (Psalm 145:3)

One generation shall praise thy works to another, and shall declare thy mighty acts. (Psalm 145:4)

All thy works shall praise thee, O LORD; and thy saints shall bless thee. (Psalm 145:10)

My mouth shall speak the praise of the LORD: and let all flesh bless his holy name for ever and ever. (Psalm 145:21)

Praise ye the LORD. Praise the LORD, O my soul. (Psalm 146:1)

While I live will I praise the LORD: I will sing praises unto my God while I have any being. (Psalm 146:2)

The LORD shall reign for ever, *even* thy God, O Zion, unto all generations. Praise ye the LORD. (Psalm 146:10)

Praise ye the LORD: for *it* *is* good to sing praises unto our God; for *it* *is* pleasant; *and* praise is comely. (Psalm 147:1)

Sing unto the LORD with thanksgiving; sing praise upon the harp unto our God. (Psalm 147:7)

Praise the LORD, O Jerusalem; praise thy God, O Zion. (Psalm 147:12)

He hath not dealt so with any nation: and *as for his* judgments, they have not known them. Praise ye the LORD. (Psalm 147:20)

Praise ye the LORD. Praise ye the LORD from the heavens: praise him in the heights. (Psalm 148:1)

Praise ye him, all his angels: praise ye him, all his hosts. (Psalm 148:2)

Praise ye him, sun and moon: praise him, all ye stars of light. (Psalm 148:3)

Praise him, ye heavens of heavens, and ye waters that *be* above the heavens. (Psalm 148:4)

Let them praise the name of the LORD: for he commanded, and they were created. (Psalm 148:5)

Praise the LORD from the earth, ye dragons, and all deeps: (Psalm 148:7)

Let them praise the name of the LORD: for his name alone is excellent; his glory *is* above the earth and heaven. (Psalm 148:13)

He also exalteth the horn of his people, the praise of all his saints; *even* of the children of Israel, a people near unto him. Praise ye the LORD. (Psalm 148:14)

Praise ye the LORD. Sing unto the LORD a new song *and* his praise in the congregation of the saints. (Psalm 149:1)

Let them praise his name in the dance: let them sing praises unto him with the timbrel and harp. (Psalm 149:3)

To execute upon them the judgment written: this honour have all his saints. Praise ye the LORD. (Psalm 149:9)

Praise ye the LORD. Praise God in his sanctuary: praise him in the firmament of his power. (Psalm 150:1)

Praise him for his mighty acts: praise him according to his excellent greatness. (Psalm 150:2)

Praise him with the sound of the trumpet: praise him with the psaltery and harp. (Psalm 150:3)

Praise him with the timbrel and dance: praise him with stringed instruments and organs. (Psalm 150:4)

Praise him upon the loud cymbals: praise him upon the high sounding cymbals. (Psalm 150:5)

Let every thing that hath breath praise the LORD. Praise ye the LORD. (Psalm 150:6)

Wisdom

By the blessing of the upright the city is **exalted**: but it is overthrown by the mouth of the wicked. (Proverbs 11:11) I bless the LORD for His Name is great and greatly to be praised.

As the fining pot for silver, and the furnace for gold; so *is* a man to his praise. Lord, let my praise to You be refined, let it be a joyful sound in Your ears, in the Name of Jesus. (Proverbs 27:21)

I praise You Lord, I do not forsake Your Word. I do not praise the wicked. (Proverbs 28:4)

I praise You, Lord, for you contend with those who contend with me. (Proverbs 28:4)

I praise You, Lord. You give me the fruit of my hands and my own works praise me in the gates. (Proverbs 31:31)

The Prophets

And in that day thou   shalt   say, O   LORD, I will praise thee: though thou wast angry with me, thine anger is turned away, and thou comfortedst me. (Isaiah 12:1)

And in that day shall ye say, Praise the LORD, call upon his name, declare his doings among the people, make

O LORD, thou *art* my God; I will exalt thee, I will praise thy name; for thou hast done wonderful *things*; *thy* counsels of old are faithfulness *and* truth. (Isaiah 25:1)

For the grave cannot praise thee, death can *not* celebrate thee: they that go down into the pit cannot hope for thy truth. So I will praise You, Lord. I will give You praise. (Isaiah 38:18)

The living, the living, he shall praise thee, as I *do* this day: the father to the children shall make known thy truth. (Isaiah 38:19)

I *am* the LORD: that *is* my name: and my glory will I not give to another, neither my praise to graven images. (Isaiah 42:8)

Sing unto the LORD a new song, *and* his praise from the end of the earth, ye that go down to the sea, and all that is therein; the isles, and the inhabitants thereof. (Isaiah 42:10)

Let them give glory unto the Lord, and declare his praise in the islands. (Isaiah 42:12)

This people have I formed for myself; they shall shew forth my praise. (Isaiah 43:21)

For my name's sake will I defer mine anger, and for my praise will I refrain for thee, that I cut thee not off. (Isaiah 48:9)

Violence shall no more be heard in thy land, wasting nor destruction within thy borders; but thou shalt call thy walls Salvation, and thy gates Praise. (Isaiah 60:18)

To appoint unto the that mourn in Zion, to give unto them beauty for ashes, the oil of joy for mourning, the garment of praise for the spirit of heaviness; that they might be called trees of righteousness, the planting of the Lord, that he might be glorified. (Isaiah 61:13)

For as the earth bringeth forth her bud, and as the garden causeth the things that are sown in it to spring forth; so the Lord GOD will cause righteousness and praise to spring forth before all the nations.. (Isaiah 61:11)

But they that have gathered it shall eat it, and praise the LORD; and they that have brought it together shall drink it in the courts of my holiness. (Isaiah 62:9)

For as the girdle cleaveth to the loins of a man, so have I caused to cleave unto me the whole houses of Israel and the whole house of Judah, saith the LORD; that they might be unto me for a people, for a name, and for a praise, and for a glory... (compare Jeremiah 13:11)

Heal me, O LORD, and I shall be healed; save me, and I shall be saved: for thou *art* my praise. (Jeremiah 17:14)

And they shall come from the cities of Judah, and from the places about Jerusalem, and from the land of Benjamin, and from the plain, and from the mountains, and from the south, bringing burnt offerings, and sacrifices, and meat offerings, and incense, and bringing sacrifices of praise, unto the house of the LORD. (Jeremiah 17:26)

Sing unto the LORD, praise ye the LORD: for he hath delivered the soul of the poor from the hand of evildoers. (Jeremiah 20:13)

For thus saith the LORD; Sing with gladness for Jacob, and shout among the chief of the nations: publish ye, praise ye, and say, O LORD, save thy people, the remnant of Israel. (Jeremiah 31:7)

And it shall be to me a name of joy, a praise and an honour before all the nations of the earth, which shall hear all the good that I do unto them: and they shall fear and tremble for all the goodness and for all the prosperity that I procure unto it. (Jeremiah 33:9)

The voice of joy, and the voice of gladness, the voice of the bridegroom, and the voice of the bride, the voice of them that shall say, Praise the LORD of hosts: for the LORD *is* good; for his mercy *endureth* for ever: *and* of them that shall bring the sacrifice of praise into the house of the LORD. For I will cause to return the captivity of the land, as at the first, saith the LORD. (Jeremiah 33:11)

How is the city of praise not left, the city of my joy! (Jeremiah 49:25). Lord, let us be the City of Praise, let us be the City of Your Joy, in the Name of Jesus.

I thank thee, and praise thee, O thou God of my fathers, who hast given me wisdom and might, and hast made known unto me now what we desired of thee; for thou hast *now* made known unto us the king's matter. (Daniel 2:23)

Now I Nebuchadnezzar praise and extol and honour the King of heaven, all whose works *are* truth, and his ways judgment: and those that walk in pride he is able to abase. (Daniel 4:37)

And ye shall eat in plenty, and be satisfied, and praise the name of the LORD your God, that hath dealt wondrously with you; and my people shall never be ashamed. (Joel 2:26)

The earth is full of his praise. (Habakkuk 3:3)

Behold, at that time I will undo all that afflict thee: and I will save her that halteth, and gather her that was driven out; and I will get them praise and fame in every land where they have been put to shame. (Zephaniah 3:19)

At that time will I bring you *again*, even in the time that I gather you: for I will make you a name and a praise among all people of the earth, when I turn back your captivity before your eyes, saith the LORD. (Zephaniah 3:20)

New Testament

...Out of the mouth of babes and sucklings thou hast perfected praise. (Matthew 21:16)

And immediately he received his sight, and followed Him, glorifying God: and all the people, when they saw *it*, gave praise unto God. (Luke 18:43)

And when he was come nigh, even now at the descent of the mount of Olives, the whole multitude of the disciples began to rejoice and praise God with a loud voice for all the mighty works that they had seen; (Luke 19:37)

Then again called they the man that was blind, and said unto him, Give God the praise: we know that this man is a sinner. (John 8:24)

Lord, let us not love the praise of men, more than the praise of God. (John 12:43)

For rulers are not a terror to good works, but to the evil. Wilt thou then not be afraid of the power? do that which is good, and thou shalt have praise of the same: (Romans 13:3)

And again, Praise the Lord, all ye Gentiles; and laud him , all ye people. (Romans 15:11)

Therefore judge nothing before the time, until the Lord come, who both will bring to the light the hidden things of darkness and will make manifest the counsels of the hearts: and then shall every man have praise of God. (1 Corinthians 4:5)

Now I praise you, brethren, that ye remember me in all things, and keep the ordinances, as I delivered *them* to you. (1 Corinthians 11:2)

And we have sent with him the brother, whose praise is the gospel throughout all the churches; (2 Corinthians 8:18)

To the praise of the glory of his grace, wherein he hath made us accepted in the beloved. (Ephesians 1:6)

That we should be to the praise of his glory, who first trusted in Christ. (Ephesians 1:12)

Which is the earnest of our inheritance until the redemption of the purchased possession, unto the praise of his glory. (Ephesians 1:14)

Being filled with the fruits of righteousness, which are by Jesus Christ, unto the glory and praise of God. (Philippians 1:11)

Finally, brethren, whatsoever things are true, whatsoever things *are* honest, whatsoever things *are* just, whatsoever   things *are* pure, whatsoever things *are* lovely, whatsoever   things *are* of   good report; if *there   be*   any   virtue,   and   if   *there   be* any praise, think on these things. (Philippians 4:8)

Saying, I will declare thy name unto my brethren, in the midst of the church will I sing praise unto thee. (Hebrews 2:12)

By him therefore let   us   offer the   sacrifice of praise to God continually, that is, the fruit of *our* lips giving thanks to his name. (Hebrews 13:15)

That the trial of your faith being much more precious than of gold that perisheth though it be tried with fire, might be found unto praise and honour and glory at the appearing of Jesus Christ: (1 Peter 1:7)

Or unto   governors, as unto   them   that   are sent by him for the   punishment of   evildoers, and for the praise of them that do well. (1 Peter 2:14)

If any   man speak, *let   him   speak* as the   oracles of God; if any   man minister, *let   him   do   it* as of the ability which God giveth: that God in all things may be glorified through Jesus Christ, to whom be praise and dominion for ever and ever. Amen. (1 Peter 4:11)

And a voice came out of the throne, saying, Praise our God, all ye his servants, and ye that fear him, both small and great. (Revelations 19:5)

And his mouth was opened immediately, and his tongue *loosed*, and he spake, and praised God. (Luke 1:64)

Glorify God

And one cried unto another, and said, Holy, holy,
holy, *is* the LORD of hosts: the whole earth *is* full of his
glory. (Isaiah 6:3)

Ye that fear the LORD, praise him; all ye the seed of
Jacob, glorify him; and fear him, all ye the seed of Israel.
(Psalm 22:23) I am the seed of Jacob, the seed of Israel. I
glorify and fear the Lord.

I praise the Lord. I call on Him in my day of trouble. The
Lord will deliver me, and I will glorify Him, forever.
(Psalm 50:15)

All nations whom thou hast made shall come and
worship before thee, O Lord; and shall glorify thy name.
(Psalm 86:9)

I will praise thee, O Lord my God, with all my heart: and
I will glorify thy name for evermore. (Psalm 86:12)

Wherefore glorify ye the LORD in the fires, *even* the
name of the LORD God of Israel in the isles of the sea.
(Isaiah 24:15)

Therefore shall the strong people glorify thee, the city of the terrible nations shall fear thee. (Isaiah 25:3)

All the flocks of Kedar shall be gathered together unto thee, the rams of Nebaioth shall minister unto thee: they shall come up with acceptance on mine altar, and I will glorify the house of my glory. (Isaiah 60:7)

And out of them shall proceed thanksgiving and the voice of them that make merry: and I will multiply them, and they shall not be few; I will also glorify them, and they shall not be small. (Jeremiah 30:19)

You're your light so shine before me, that they may your good works, and glorify your Father which is in heaven. (Matthew 5:16)

Father, glorify they name. Then came there a voice from heaven, saying, I have both glorified it, and will glorify it again. (John 12:28)

If God be glorified in him, God shall also glorify him in himself, and shall straightway glorify him. (John 13:32) I glorify, I magnify, I lift up the Name of the Lord for He is worthy to be praised.

These words spake Jesus, and lifted up his eyes to heaven, and said, Father, the hour is come; glorify thy Son, that thy Son also may glorify thee; (John 17:1)

And now, O Father, florify thou me with thine own self with the glory which I had with thee before the world was. (John 17:5)

That ye may with one mind *and* one mouth glorify God, even the Father of our Lord Jesus Christ. (Romans 15:6)

And that the Gentiles might glorify God for his mercy; as it is written, for this cause I will confess to thee among the Gentiles, and sing unto thy name. (Romans 15:9)

Fo ye are bought with a price: therefore glorify God in your body, and in your spirit, w hich are God's. (1 Corinthians 6:20)

Whiles by the experiment of this ministration they glorify God for your professed subjection unto the gospel of Christ, and for your liberal distribution unto them, and unto all *men*; (2 Corinthians 9:13)

Having your conversation honest among the Gentiles: th at, whereas they speak against you as evildoers, they may by *your* good works, which they shall behold, glorify God in the day of visitation. (1 Peter 2:12)

Yet if *any man suffer* as a Christian, let him not be ashamed; but let him glorify God on this behalf. (1 Peter 4:16)

Who shall not fear thee, O Lord, and glorify thy name? for *thou* only *art* holy: for all nations shall come and worship before thee; for thy judgments are made manifest. (Revelations 15:4)

Then Moses said unto Aaron, This *is* *it* that the LORD spake, saying, I will be sanctified in them that come nigh me, and before all the people I will be glorified. And Aaron held his peace. (Leviticus 10:3)

Thou hast increased the nation, O LORD, thou hast increased the nation: thou art glorified: thou hadst removed *it* far *unto* all the ends of the earth. (Isaiah 26:15) I praise You Lord, for you have increased me, my family, my city and my nation. You are glorified, O Lord.

Sing, O ye heavens; for the LORD hath done *it*: shout, ye lower parts of the earth: break forth into singing, ye mountains, O forest, and every tree therein: for the LORD hath redeemed Jacob, and glorified himself in Israel. (Isaiah 44:23)

And said unto me, Thou *art* my servant, O Israel, in whom I will be glorified.(Isaiah 49:3) Glorify Yourself in me, through me, O Lord.

Behold, thou shalt call a nation *that* thou knowest not, and nations *that* knew thee not thee shall run unto thee because of the LORD thy God, and for the Holy One of Israel; for he hath glorified thee. (Isaiah 55:5)

Surely the isles shall wait for me, and the ships of Tarshish first, to bring thy sons from far, their silver and their gold with them, unto the name of the LORD thy God, and to the Holy One of Israel, because he hath glorified thee. (Isaiah 60:9)

Thy people also *shall be* all righteous: they shall inherit the land for ever, the branch of my planting, the work of my hands, that I may be glorified. (Isaiah 60:21)

To appoint unto them that mourn in Zion, to give unto them beauty for ashes, the oil of joy for mourning, the garment of praise for the spirit of heaviness; that they might be called trees of righteousness, the planting of the LORD, that he might be glorified. (Isaiah 61:3)

Hear the word of the LORD, ye that tremble at his word; Your brethren that hated you, that cast you out for my name's sake, said, Let the LORD be glorified: but he shall appear to your joy, and they shall be ashamed. (Isaiah 66:5)

And say, Thus saith the Lord GOD; Behold, I *am* against thee, O Zidon; and I will be glorified in the midst of thee: and they shall know that I *am* the LORD, when I shall have executed judgments in her, and shall be sanctified in her. (Ezekiel 28:22)

I shall be glorified, saith the Lord GOD. (Ezekiel 39:13)

But when the multitudes saw *it*, they marvelled, and glorified God, which had given such power unto men. (Matthew 9:8)

Insomuch that the multitude wondered, when they saw the dumb to speak, the maimed to be whole, the lame to walk, and the blind to see: and they glorified the God of Israel. (Matthew 15:31)

And immediately he arose, took up the bed, and went forth before them all; insomuch that they were all amazed, and glorified God, saying, We never saw it on this fashion. (Mark 2:12)

And he taught in their synagogues, being glorified of all. (Luke 4:15)

And they were all amazed, and they glorified God, and were filled with fear, saying, We have seen strange things to day. (Luke 5:26)

And there came a fear on all: and they glorified God, saying, that a great prophet is risen up among us, and that God hath visited his people. (Luke 7:16)

He laid his hands on her: and immediately she was made straight, and glorified God. (Luke 13:13)

And one of them, when he saw that he was healed, turned back, and with a loud voice glorified God, (Luke 17:15)

Now when the centurion saw what was done, he glorified God, saying, Certainly this was a righteous man. (Luke 23:47)

But this spake he of the Spirit, which they that believe on him should receive; for the Holy Ghost was not yet *given*; because that Jesus was not yet glorified.(John 7:39)

When Jesus heard *that*, this sickness is not unto death, but for the glory of God, that the Son of God might be glorified. (John 11:4)

These things understood not his disciples at the first: but when Jesus was glorified, then remembered they that these things were written of him, and *that* they had done these things unto him. (John 12:6)

And Jesus answered them, saying, The hour is   come, that the Son of man should be glorified. (John 12:23)

Father, glorify thy name. then came there a voice from heaven, *saying,* I have both gloried it and will glorify *it* again. (John 12:28)

Therefore, when he was gone out, Jesus said, Now is the Son of man glorified, and God is glorified in him. (John 13:31)

If God be glorified in him, God shall also glorify him in himself, and shall straightway glorify him (John 13:32)

And whatsoever ye   shall   ask in my name, that will   I do, that the Father may   be glorified in the Son.   (John 14:13)

Herein is my Father glorified, that ye bear much fruit; so shall ye be my disciples. (John 15:8)

I have glorified thee on the earth: I have finished the work which thou gavest me to do. (John 17:4)

And all mine are thine, and thine   are   mine; and I   am glorified in them. (John 17:10)

The God of Abraham, and of Isaac; and of Jacob, the God of our fathers, hath glorified his Son Jesus; whom ye delivered up, and denied him in the presence of Pilate, when he was determined to let *him* go. (Acts 3:13)

So when they had further threatened them, they let them go, finding nothing how they might punish them, because of the people for all *men* glorified God for that which was done. (Acts 4:21)

When they heard these things, they held their peace, and glorified God, saying, Then hath God also to the Gentiles granted repentance unto life. (Acts 11:18)

And when the Gentiles heard this, they were glad, and glorified the word of the Lord: and as many as were ordained to eternal life believed. (Acts 13:48)

And when they heard *it*, they glorified the Lord, and aid unto him, Thou seest, brother, how many thousands of Jews there are which believe; and they are all zealous of the law: (Acts 21:20)

And if children, then heirs; heirs of God, and joint-heirs with Christ; if so be that we suffer with *him*, that we may be also **glorified** together. (Romans 8:17)

Moreover whom he did predestinate, them he also called: and whom he called, them he also justified: and whom he justified, he also glorified. (Romans 8:30)

And they **glorified** God in me. (Galatians 1:24)

When he shall come to be glorified in his saints, and to he admired in all them that believe (because our testimony among you was believed) in that day. (2 Thessalonians 1:10)

That the name of our Lord Jesus Christ may be glorified in you, and ye in him, according, to the grace of our God and the Lord Jesus Christ. (2 Thessalonians 1:12)

Finally, brethren, pray for us, that the word of the Lord may have *free* course, and be glorified, even as *it is* with you. (2 Thessalonians 3:1)

So also Christ glorified not himself to be man an high priest; but he that said unto him, Thou art my Son, to day have I begotten thee. (Hebrews 5:5)

If any man speak, *let him speak* as the oracles of God; if any man minister, *let him do it* as of the ability which God giveth: that God in all things may be glorified through Jesus Christ, to whom be praise and dominion for ever and ever. Amen. (1 Peter 4:11)

If ye be reproached for the name of Christ, happy *are* ye; for the spirit of glory and of God resteth upon you: on their part he is evil spoken of, but on your part he is glorified. (1 Peter 4:14)

Magnify

♫ Be magnified, O Lord
You are highly exalted
And there is nothing You can't do
O Lord, my eyes are on You
Be magnified
O Lord, be magnified *(Don Moen)*

And the LORD said unto Joshua, This day will I begin to magnify thee in the sight of all Israel, that they may know that, as I was with Moses, *so* I will be with thee. (Joshua 3:7)

What *is* man, that though shouldest magnify him? And that thou shouldest set thing heart upon him? (Job 7:17)

If indeed ye ill magnify *yourselves* against me, and plead against me my reproach: (Job 19:5)

Remember that thou magnify his work, which men behold. (Job 36:24)

O magnify the LORD with me, and let us exalt his name together. (Psalm 34:3)

Let them be ashamed and brought to confusion together that rejoice at mine hurt: let them be clothed with *shame* and dishonour that magnify themselves against me. (Psalm 35:26)

I will praise the name of God with a song, and will magnify him with thanksgiving. (Psalm 69:30)

The LORD is well pleased for his righteousness' sake; he will magnify the law, and make *it* honourable. (Isaiah 42:21)

Thus will I magnify myself, and sanctify myself; and I will be known in the eyes of many nations, and they shall know that I *am* the LORD. (Ezekiel 38:23)

And through his policy also he shall cause craft to prosper in his hand; and he shall magnify *himself* in his heart, and by peace shall destroy many: he shall also stand up against the Prince of princes; but he shall be broken without hand. (Daniel 8:25)

The LORD also shall save the tents of Judah first, that the glory of the house of David and the glory of the inhabitants of Jerusalem. We magnify God; we do not magnify ourselves. (compare Zechariah 12:7)

And Mary said, My soul doth magnify the Lord, (Luke 1:46)

For they heard them speak with tongues, and magnify God. (Acts 10:46)

Behold now, thy servant hath found grace in thy sight, and thou hast magnified thy mercy, which thou hast shewed unto me in saving my life; (Genesis 19:19A) I magnify You, Lord God; it is because of You that I live.

On that day the LORD magnified Joshua in the sight of all Israel; and they feared him, as they feared Moses, all the days of his life. (Joshua 4:14) Lord, You are great; You can magnify and You can diminish.

And let thy name be magnified for ever, saying, The LORD of hosts is the God over Israel: and let the house of thy servant David be established before thee. (2 Samuel 7:26)

Let it even be established, that thy name may be magnified for ever, saying, The LORD of hosts is the God of Israel, *even* a God to Israel: and *let* the house of David thy servant *be* established before thee. (1 Chronicles 17:24)

And the Lord magnified Solomon exceedingly in the sight of all Israel, and bestowed up him *such* royal majesty as had not been on any king before him in Israel. (1 Chronicles 29:25)

As the Lord God was with Solomon, and magnified him exceedingly, I magnify You, Lord God. (see 2 Chronicles 1:1)

And many brought gifts unto the LORD to Jerusalem, and presents to Hezekiah king of Judah: so that he was magnified in the sight of all nations from thenceforth. (2 Chronicles 32:23)

Let them shout for joy, and be glad, that favour my righteous cause: yea, let them say continually, Let the

LORD be magnified, which hath pleasure in the prosperity of his servant. (Psalm 35:27)

Let all those that seek thee rejoice and be glad in thee: let such as love thy salvation say continually, The LORD be magnified. (Psalm 40:16)

Let all those that seek thee rejoice and be glad in thee: and let such as love thy salvation say continually, Let God be magnified. (Psalm 70:4)

I will worship toward thy holy temple, and praise thy name for thy lovingkindness and for thy truth: for thou hast magnified thy word above all thy name. (Psalm 138:2)

And your eyes shall see, and ye shall say, The LORD will be magnified from the border of Israel.(Malachi 1:5)

And of the rest durst no man join himself to them: but the people magnified them. (Acts 5:13)

Fear fell on the Greeks and Jews dwelling in Ephesus, and the name of the Lord Jesus was magnified. (see Acts 19:16-17)

According to my earnest expectation and my hope, *that* in nothing I shall be ashamed, but that with all boldness, as always, so no also Christ shall be magnified in my body, whether *it be* by life, or by death. (Philemon 1:20)

Majesty

♪♪ O Lord, our Lord, how majestic is your name in all
the earth.
O Lord, our Lord, how majestic is your name in all the
earth.
O Lord, we praise your name.
O Lord, we magnify your name:
Prince of Peace, mighty God;
O Lord God Almighty. (Michael W. Smith)

Thine, O LORD, *is* the greatness, and the power, and the
glory, and the victory, and the majesty: for all *that is* in
the heaven and in the earth *is* *thine*; thine *is* the
kingdom, O LORD, and thou art exalted as head above
all. (1 Chronicles 29:11)

And the LORD magnified Solomon exceedingly in the
sight of all Israel, and bestowed upon him *such* royal
majesty as had not been on any king before in Israel. (1
Chronicles 20:25)

When he shewed the riches of his glorious kingdom and
the honour of his excellent majesty many days, *even* an
hundred and fourscore days. (Esther 1:4)

Fair weather cometh out of the north: with God *is* terrible majesty. (Job 37:22)

Deck thyself now *with* majesty and excellency; and array thyself with glory and beauty. (Job 40:10)

His glory is great in thy salvation: honour and majesty hast thou laid upon him. (Psalm 21:5)

The voice of the LORD *is* powerful; the voice of the LORD *is* full of majesty. (Psalm 29:4)

Gird thy sword upon *thy* thigh, O *most* mighty, with thy glory and thy majesty. (Psalm 45:3)

And in thy majesty ride prosperously because of truth and meekness *and* righteousness; and thy right hand shall teach thee terrible things. (Psalm 45:4)

The LORD reigneth, he is clothed with majesty; the LORD is clothed with strength, *wherewith* he hath girded himself: the world also is stablished, that it cannot be moved. Thy throne is established of old; thou art from everlasting . (Psalm 93:1-2)

Honour and majesty *are* before him; strength and beauty *are* in his sanctuary. (Psalm 96:6)

Bless the LORD, O my soul. O LORD my God, thou art very great; thou art clothed with honour and majesty. (Psalm 104:1)

I will speak of the glorious honour of thy majesty, and of thy wondrous works. (Psalm 145:5)

To make known to the sons of men his mighty acts, and the glorious majesty of his kingdom. (Psalm 145:12)

Enter into the rock, and hide thee in the dust, for fear of the LORD, and for the glory of his majesty. (Isaiah 2:10)

And they shall go into the holes of the rocks, and into the caves of the earth, for fear of the LORD, and for the glory of his majesty, when he ariseth to shake terribly the earth.(Isaiah 2:19)

To go into the clefts of the rocks, and into the tops of the ragged rocks, for fear of the LORD, and for the glory of his majesty, when he ariseth to shake terribly the earth. (Isaiah 2:21)

They shall lift up their voice, they shall sing for the majesty of the LORD, they shall cry aloud from the sea. (Isaiah 24:14)

Let favour be shewed to the wicked, *yet* will he not learn righteousness: in the land of uprightness will he deal unjustly, and will not behold the majesty of the LORD. (Isaiah 26:10)

As for the beauty of his ornament, he set it in majesty: but they made the images of their abominations *and* of their detestable things therin: therefore have I set it far from them. (Ezekiel 7:20)

The king spake and said, Is not this great Babylon, that I have built for the house of the kingdom by the might of my power, and for the honour of my majesty? (Daniel 4:30)

And he (Nebuchadnezzar) shall stand and feed in the strength of the LORD, in the majesty of the name of the LORD his God; and they shall abide: for now shall he be great unto the ends of the earth. (Micah 5:4)

Who being the brightness of *his* glory, and the express image of his person, and upholding all things by the word of his power, when he had by himself purged out sins, sat down on the right hand of the Majesty on high; (Hebrews 1:3)

Now of the things which we have spoken *this* *is* the sum: We have such an high priest, who is set on the right hand of the throne of the Majesty in the heavens; (Hebrews 8:1)

For we have not followed cunningly devised fables, when we made known unto you the power and the coming of our Lord Jesus Christ, but were eyewitnesses of his majesty. (1 Peter 1:16)

To the only wise God our Saviour, *be* glory and majesty, dominion and power both now and ever. Amen. (Jude 1:25)

After it a voice roars; He thunders with His majestic voice, And He does not restrain them when His voice is heard. (Job 37:4)

Beauty

♫ Cause all my life You have been faithful
And all my life You have been so, so good
With every breath that I am able
Oh, I will sing of the goodness of God. (Bethel
Music)

One thing I ask from the LORD... that I may dwell in the house of the LORD all the days of my life, to gaze upon the beauty of the LORD and to seek Him in His temple. (Psalm 27:4)

Let the beauty of the LORD our God be upon us, and establish the work of our hands... (Psalm 90:17)

Worship the LORD in the beauty of holiness; tremble before Him, all the earth. (Psalm 96:9)

Out of Zion, the perfection of beauty, God shines forth. (Psalm 50:2)

On the glorious splendor of Your majesty, and on Your wondrous works, I will meditate. (Psalm 145:5)

Your eyes will behold the King in His beauty... (Isaiah 33:17)

...to give them beauty for ashes, the oil of joy for mourning... that He may be glorified. (Isaiah 61:3)

His splendor covered the heavens, and the earth was full of His praise. His brightness was like the light... (Habakkuk 3:3-4)

You are clothed with splendor and majesty, covering Yourself with light as with a garment. (Psalm 104:1-2)

Ascribe to the LORD the glory due His name; worship the LORD in the splendor of holiness. (Psalm 29:2)

Worship the LORD in the splendid beauty of holiness. (1 Chronicles 16:29)

We all... beholding the glory of the Lord, are being transformed into the same image from glory to glory... (2 Corinthians 3:18)

The city has no need of sun or moon to shine on it, for the glory of God gives it light... (Revelation 21:23)

He who sat there had the appearance of jasper and ruby, and around the throne was a rainbow that shone like an emerald. (Revelation 4:3)

Strength

God is our refuge and strength, a very present help in trouble. (Psalm 46:1)

He gives power to the faint, and to him who has no might He increases strength. (Isaiah 40:29)

The joy of the LORD is my strength. (see, Nehemiah 8:10)

I love You, O LORD, my strength. The LORD is my rock and my fortress and my deliverer... (Psalm 18:1-2)

The LORD is my strength and my shield; in Him my heart trusts, and I am helped. (Psalm 28:7)

Fear not, for I am with you... I will strengthen you, I will help you, I will uphold you with my righteous right hand. (Isaiah 41:10)

The LORD is my strength and my song, and He has become my salvation. (Exodus 15:2)

The LORD God is my strength; He makes my feet like the deer's; He enables me to tread on the heights. (Habakkuk 3:19)

It is God who arms me with strength and keeps my way secure. (2 Samuel 22:33)

Seek the LORD and His strength; seek His presence continually. (1 Chronicles 16:11)

I can do all things through Christ who strengthens me. (Philippians 4:13)

Be strong in the Lord and in the strength of His might. (Ephesians 6:10)

"My grace is sufficient for you, for My power is made perfect in weakness."... When I am weak, then I am strong. (2 Corinthians 12:9-10)

My flesh and my heart may fail, but God is the strength of my heart and my portion forever. (Psalm 73:26)

Be strong and courageous... for it is the LORD your God who goes with you; He will not leave you or forsake you. (Deuteronomy 31:6)

Whoever serves, do so with the strength God supplies... (1 Peter 4:11)

For he strengthens the bars of your gates; he blesses your children within you.(Psalm 147:13 ESV)

He trains my hands for battle; he strengthens my arm to draw a bronze bow. (2 Samuel 22:35 NLT)

He trains my hands for battle; he strengthens my arm to draw a bronze bow. (Psalm 18:34 NLT)

Strengthened with all power, according to His glorious might, for all endurance and patience with joy. (Colossians 1:11)

The LORD is the stronghold of my life; of whom shall I be afraid? (Psalm 27:1)

Ascribe ye strength unto God: his excellency *is* over Israel, and his strength *is* in the clouds. (Psalm 68:34)

Surely God is my salvation; I will trust and not be afraid. The LORD Himself is my strength and my song. (Isaiah 12:2)

God's Power

Thou art worthy, O Lord, to receive glory and honour and power: for thou hast created all things, and for thy pleasure they are and were created. (Revelations 4:11)

God's power isn't abstract. In Scripture it always does something: creates worlds, splits seas, silences enemies, lifts the humble, resurrects the dead, and strengthens people who barely have breath left. It is power that moves toward us, not away from us.

Ah, Lord GOD! It is You who made the heavens and the earth by Your great power and by Your outstretched arm. Nothing is too hard for You. (Jeremiah 32:17)

Indeed, these are just the edges of His ways; how faint the whisper we hear of Him. Who then can understand the thunder of His power? (Job 26:14)

Once God has spoken; twice have I heard this: that power belongs to God. (Psalm 62:11)

Great is our Lord and mighty in power; His understanding has no limit. (Psalm 147:5)

The LORD is the everlasting God... He does not faint or grow weary; His understanding is unsearchable. (Isaiah 40:28)

The Lord acts, and who can reverse it? (compare Isaiah 43:13)

[That you may know] the immeasurable greatness of His power toward us who believe, according to the working of His great might that He worked in Christ when He raised Him from the dead. (Ephesians 1:19-20)

His invisible attributes, namely His eternal power and divine nature, have been clearly perceived... in the things that have been made. (Romans 1:20)

For nothing will be impossible with God. (Luke 1:37)

With man this is impossible, but with God all things are possible. (Matthew 19:26)

Blessed be the name of God forever and ever, to whom belong wisdom and might. He changes times and seasons... (Daniel 2:20-21)

For this purpose I raised you up, to show you My power... (Exodus 9:16)

The kingdom of God does not consist in talk but in power. (1 Corinthians 4:20)

He rescued me from my powerful enemy, from foes too strong for me. (Psalm 18:17)

♫ All honor
All glory
All power
To You (x4)

Holy Father we worship You
Precious Jesus our Saviour

Holy spirit we wait on You
Holy spirit we wait on You
Holy spirit we wait on You

For fire. (*All Honor*, Ron Kenoly)

God gave us a spirit not of fear but of power and love and self-control. (2 Timothy 1:7)

Hallelujah! For the Lord our God the Almighty reigns. (Revelation 19:6)

Yours, O LORD, is the greatness and the power and the glory and the victory and the majesty...(1 Chronicles 29:11)

Who by His power formed the mountains, being girded with might. (Psalm 65:6)

That I may know Him and the power of His resurrection... (Philippians 3:10)

♫ Because God is the greatest power
We shall never, never be defeated
Because God is the greatest power
We shall never, never be defeated
Because God is the greatest power
We shall never, never be defeated

I shall rise I shall be
I shall go with victory
No weapon formed against me
Will ever overtake me. (***Never Be Defeated***, Rich Tolbert, Jr and Jabari Johnson)

And now these three remain: faith, hope and love. But the greatest of these is love. (1 Corinthians 13:13)

Love is the greatest power; and God is Love.

Exalt Him

You are highly exalted. There is nothing that you can't do. O Lord, my eyes are on You.

The LORD *is* my strength and song, and he is become my salvation: he *is* my God, and I will prepare him an habitation; my father's God, and I will exalt him. (Exodus 15:2)

The adversaries of the LORD shall be broken to pieces; out of heaven shall he thunder upon them: the LORD shall judge the ends of the earth; and he shall give strength unto his king, and exalt the horn of his anointed. (1 Samuel 2:10)

O magnify the LORD with me, and let us exalt his name together. (Psalm 34:3)

Wait on the LORD, and keep his way, and he shall exalt thee to inherit the land: when the wicked are cut off, thou shalt see *it*. (Psalm 37:34)

He ruleth by his power for ever; his eyes behold the nations: let not the rebellious exalt themselves. Selah. (Psalm 66:7)

But my horn shalt thou exalt like *the horn of* an unicorn: I shall be anointed with fresh oil. (Psalm 92:10)

Exalt ye the LORD our God, and worship at his footstool; *for* he *is* holy. (Psalm 99:5)

Exalt the LORD our God, and worship at his holy hill; for the LORD our God *is* holy. (Psalm 99:9)

Let them exalt him also in the congregation of the people, and praise him in the assembly of the elders. (Psalm 107:32)

Thou *art* my God, and I will praise thee: *thou art* my God, I will exalt thee. (Psalm 118:28)

Exalt her, and she shall promote thee: she shall bring thee to honour, when thou dost embrace her. (Proverbs 4:8) I exalt the Lord. I lift Him up and it is the Lord who gives promotion.

Lift ye up a banner upon the high mountain, exalt the voice unto them, shake the hand, that they may go into the gates of the nobles. (Isaiah 13:2)

For thou hast said in thine heart, I will ascend into heaven, I will exalt my throne above the stars of God: I will sit also upon the mount of the congregation, in the sides of the north: (Isaiah 14:13)

O LORD, thou *art* my God; I will exalt thee, I will praise thy name; for thou hast done wonderful *things; thy* counsels of old *are* faithfulness *and* truth. (Isaiah 25:1)

Thus saith the Lord GOD; Remove the diadem, and take off the crown: this *shall* not *be* the same: exalt *him that is* low, and abase *him that is* high. (Ezekiel 21:26)

It shall be the basest of the kingdoms; neither shall it exalt itself any more above the nations: for I will diminish them, that they shall no more rule over the nations. (Ezekiel 29:15)

To the end that none of all the trees by the waters exalt themselves for their height, neither shoot up their top among the thick boughs, neither their trees stand up in their height, all that drink water: for they are all delivered unto death, to the nether parts of the earth, in the midst of the children of men, with them that go down to the pit. (Ezekiel 31:14)

And in those times there shall many stand up against the king of the south: also the robbers of thy people shall exalt themselves to establish the vision; but they shall fall. (Daniel 11:14)

And the king shall do according to his will; and he shall exalt himself, and magnify himself above every god, and shall speak marvellous things against the God of gods, and shall prosper till the indignation be accomplished: for that that is determined shall be done. (Daniel 11:36)

Though thou exalt *thyself* as the eagle, and though thou set thy nest among the stars, thence will I bring thee down, saith the LORD. (Obadiah 1:4)

Humble   yourselves therefore under the mighty hand of God, that he may exalt you in due time. (1 Peter 5:6)

He shall   pour the   water out of his   buckets, and   his seed *shall   be* in many waters, and his   king shall   be higher than   Agag, and his   kingdom shall   be exalted. (Numbers 24:7)

And Hannah prayed, and said, My heart rejoiceth in the LORD, mine horn is exalted in the LORD: my mouth is enlarged over mine   enemies; because I   rejoice in   thy salvation. (1 Samuel 2:1)

And David perceived that the   LORD had   established him king over Israel, and   that he   had exalted his kingdom for his people Israel's sake.(2 Samuel 5:12)

The LORD liveth; and blessed *be* my rock; and exalted be the God of the rock of my salvation. (2 Samuel 22:47)

I exalted You as King O God. You are the Prince of Peace and King over all kings. (compare 1 King 14:7)

Whom hast   thou   reproached and   blasphemed? and against whom hast   thou exalted *thy* voice, and   lifted up thine   eyes on   high? *even* against the   Holy *One* of Israel. (1 Kings 16:2)

Thine, O LORD, *is* the greatness, and the power, and the glory, and the victory, and the majesty: for all *that is* in the   heaven and in   the   earth *is   thine*; thine *is* the kingdom, O LORD, and thou art exalted as head above all. (1 Chronicles 29:11)

Then the   Levites…said, Stand   up *and* bless the LORD your God for ever and ever: and blessed be thy glorious name, which   is exalted above all blessing and praise. (Nehemiah 9:5)

He withdraweth not his eyes from the righteous: but with kings *are they* on the throne; yea, he doth establish them for ever, and they are exalted. (Job 36:7)

I exalt You, O Lord, for You did not allow my enemy to be exalted over me. (compare Psalm 13:2)

The LORD liveth; and blessed *be* my rock; and let the God of my salvation be exalted (Psalm 18:46).

Be thou exalted, LORD, in thine own strength: *so* will we sing and praise thy power. (Psalm 21:13)

Be still, and know that I *am* God: I will be exalted among the heathen, I will be exalted in the earth. (Psalm 46:10)

The princes of the people are gathered together, *even* the people of the God of Abraham: for the shields of the earth *belong* unto God: he is greatly exalted. (Psalm 47:9)

Be   thou exalted, O   God, above the   heavens; *let* thy glory *be* above all the earth. (Psalm 57:5)

Be   thou exalted, O   God, above the   heavens: *let* thy glory *be* above all the earth. (Psalm 57:11)

All the horns of the wicked also will I cut off; *but* the horns of the righteous shall be exalted. (Psalm 75:10)

In thy name shall they rejoice all the day: and in thy righteousness shall they be exalted. (Psalm 89:16)

For thou *art* the glory of their strength: and in thy favour our horn shall be exalted. (Psalm 89:17)

Then thou spakest in vision to thy holy one, and saidst, I have laid help upon *one that is* mighty; I have exalted *one* chosen out of the people. (Psalm 89:19)

But my faithfulness and my mercy *shall be* with him: and in my name shall his horn be exalted. (Psalm 89:24)

For thou, LORD, *art* high above all the earth: thou art exalted far above all gods. (Psalm 97:9)

Be thou exalted, O God, above the heavens: and thy glory above all the earth; (Psalm 108:5)

He hath dispersed, he hath given to the poor; his righteousness endureth for ever; his horn shall be exalted with honour. (Psalm 112:9)

The right hand of the LORD is exalted: the right hand of the LORD doeth valiantly. (Psalm 118:16)

And it shall come to pass in the last days, *that* the mountain of the LORD'S house shall be established in the top of the mountains, and shall be exalted above the hills; and all nations shall flow unto it. (Isaiah 2:2)

The lofty looks of man shall be humbled, and the haughtiness of men shall be bowed down, and the LORD alone shall be exalted in that day. (Isaiah 2:11)

And the loftiness of man shall be bowed down, and the haughtiness of men shall be made low: and the LORD alone shall be exalted in that day. (Isaiah 2:17)

But the LORD of hosts shall be exalted in judgment, and God that is holy shall be sanctified in righteousness. (Isaiah 5:16)

And in that day shall ye say, Praise the LORD, call upon his name, declare his doings among the people, make mention that his name is exalted. (Isaiah 12:4)

And therefore will the LORD wait, that he may be gracious unto you, and therefore will he be exalted, that he may have mercy upon you: for the LORD *is* a God of judgment: blessed *are* all they that wait for him. (Isaiah 30:18)

The LORD is exalted; for he dwelleth on high: he hath filled Zion with judgment and righteousness. (Isaiah 33:5)

Now will I rise, saith the LORD; now will I be exalted; ow will I lift up myself. (Isaiah 33:10)

Whom hast thou reproached and blasphemed? and against whom hast thou exalted *thy* voice, and lifted up thine eyes on high? *even* against the Holy One of Israel. (Isaiah 37:23)

Every valley shall be exalted, and every mountain and hill shall be made low: and the crooked shall be made straight, and the rough places plain: (Isaiah 40:4)

And I will make all my mountains a way, and my highways shall be exalted. (Isaiah 49:11)

Behold, my servant shall deal prudently, he shall be exalted and extolled, and be very high. (Isaiah 52:13)

And all the trees of the field shall know that I the LORD have brought down the high tree, have exalted the low tree, have dried up the green tree, and have made the dry tree to flourish: I the LORD have spoken and have done *it*. (Ezekiel 17:24)

And she had strong rods for the sceptres of them that bare rule, and her stature was exalted among the thick branches, and she appeared in her height with the multitude of her branches. (Ezekiel 19:11)

Therefore his height was exalted above all the trees of the field, and his boughs were multiplied, and his branches became long because of the multitude of waters, when he shot forth. (Ezekiel 31:5)

But in the last days it shall come to pass, *that* the mountain of the house of the LORD shall be established in the top of the mountains, and it shall be exalted above the hills; and people shall flow unto it. (Micah 4:1)

Extol the Lord

I will **extol** thee, O LORD; for thou hast lifted me up, and hast not made my foes to rejoice over me. (Psalm 30:1)

Sing unto God, sing praises to his name: **extol** him that rideth upon the heavens by his name JAH, and rejoice before him. (Psalm 68:4)

I will **extol** thee, my God, O king; and I will bless thy name for ever and ever. (Psalm 145:1)

Now I Nebuchadnezzar praise and extol and honour the King of heaven, all whose works *are* truth, and his ways judgment: and those that walk in pride he is able to abases. (Daniel 4:37)

I cried unto him with my mouth, and he was **extolled** with my tongue. (Psalm 66:17)

Behold, my servant shall deal prudently, he shall be exalted and **extolled**, and be very high. (Isaiah 52:13)

Praise Lyrics ♫

My Jesus, my Savior Lord, there is none like You. All of
my days I want to praise
The wonders of Your mighty love.

My comfort, my shelter. Tower of refuge and strength.
Let every breath, all that I am
Never cease to worship You. (**Shout to the Lord**,
Darlene Zscchech)

Lord I lift your name on high
Lord I love to sing your praises
I'm so glad you are in my life
I'm so glad you came to save us

You came from heaven to earth, to show the way. From
the earth to the cross, my debt to pay. From the cross to
the grave, from the grave to the sky
Lord I lift your name on high. (**Lord, I Lift Your Name
on High,** Rick Doyle Founds)

Majesty Majesty, Majesty
Your grace has found me just as I am

Empty handed but alive in Your hands
We're singing Majesty, we're singing Majesty
Forever, forever I am changed by Your love
In the presence of Your Majesty (*Majesty*, Martin
Smith, Stuart David Garrad)

Great is Thy faithfulnessGreat is Thy faithfulness.
Morning by morning new mercies I see. All I have
needed Thy hand hath provided. Great is Thy
faithfulness, Lord, unto me.(*Great Is Thy Faithfulness*,
Adam Anders, Thomas Chisholm, William Runyan)

O Lord, my God, when I in awesome wonder
Consider all the worlds Thy Hands have made.
I see the stars, I hear the rolling thunder
Thy power throughout the universe displayed
Then sings my soul, My Saviour God, to Thee
How great Thou art, how great Thou art. (*How Great
Thou Art*, Stuart Keene Hine)

Waymaker, Miracle Worker, Promise Keeper, Light in
the darkness. My God
That is who You are. (*Waymaker*, Osinachi Kalu Okoro
Egbu)

Cause you are perfect in all of your ways
You are perfect in all of your ways
You are perfect in all of your ways to us

You are perfect in all of your ways
You are perfect in all of your ways
You are perfect in all of your ways to us (***Good Good Father***, Chris Tomlin)

Every praise is to our God.
Every word of worship with one accord
Every praise every praise is to our God.
Sing hallelujah to our God
Glory hallelujah is due our God
Every praise every praise is to our God (***Every Praise,*** Hezekiah Walker, John David Bratton)

Lord, You are good
And Your mercy endureth forever
Lord, You are good
And Your mercy endureth forever

People from every nation and tongue
From generation to generation..

You are good all the time,

All the time You are Good. (***You Are Good*** (Israel Houghton)

I will bless the Lord
Oh my soul
Bless the lord with me
He is the Lord of all

Forever more
Bless the Lord with me. (Best Praise, Ay Ron Ronell
Lewis, James Howard Iii Fortune, Cheryl Fortune)

Praise the Lord, I've been born again. (Elevation)

How great is our God
Sing with me
How great is our God
And all will see
How great, how great is our God.
(***How Great Is Our God***, Chris Tomlin)

I will exalt You
I will exalt You
I will exalt You
You are my God

My hiding place
My safe refuge
My treasure Lord You are
My friend and King
Anointed One
Most Holy (***I Will Exalt You***, William Murphy, (Bethel)

Hallelujah for saving me
Hallelujah for healing my body
Hallelujah for joy You bring
Let everything that hath breath give you praise (in the
morning)

Praise (in the noonday.
Praise (in the midnight)
Let everything that hath breath give it to You *(Let
Everything That Has Breath*, Matt Redman)

My hallelujah belongs to You
My hallelujah belongs to You
My hallelujah belongs to You
My hallelujah belongs to You
You deserve it
You deserve it
You deserve it
You deserve it
My hallelujah (*You Deserve It*, JJ Hairston)

You freed the captives then, You're freeing hearts
right now
You are the same God, You are the same God
You touched the lepers then, I feel Your touch right
now
You are the same God, You are the same God
Never changes, oh forever
We feel You now
You are the same God, You are the same God (*Same
God,* Elevation)

Take the shackles off my feet so I can dance

I just want to praise You
I just want to praise You
You broke the chains now I can lift my hands
And I'm gonna praise You
Said I'm gonna praise You (*I Just Want to Praise You*, Natalie Grant & Mary Mary)

Hosanna
Blessed be the rock
Blessed be the rock of my salvation
Hosanna
Blessed be the rock
Blessed be the rock of my salvation

Oh magnify the Lord
For He is worthy to be praised
Oh magnify the Lord
For He is worthy to be praised (*Oh Magnify the Lord*, Jonathan Butler)

You are the God
Who was, Who is and is to come
Jesus, Jesus
And in You I trust
My life is in Your Hands
Jesus, You are the Miracle working God

You are Yahweh, eh eh eh
You are Yahweh

You are Yahweh, eh eh eh
You are Yahweh
You are Yahweh
Alpha and Omega
You are Yahweh
Alpha and Omega(You Are Yahweh,

Saviour, he can move the mountains
My God is mighty to save
He is mighty to save
Forever Author of Salvation
He rose and conquered the grave
Jesus conquered the grave (*Mighty to Save,*
Hillsong**)**

I sing praises to Your Name

O Lord. Praises to Your Name, O Lord. For Your
Name is great and greatly to be praised. (*I Sing
Praises to Your Name,* Terry Macalmon, Hillsong)

With a grateful heart, I lift my hands to You
Proclaiming Lord, You reign
With a grateful heart, I lift my hands to You
Proclaiming Lord, You reign
(Lord, You reign!)
Great are You, Lord
You're greatly to be praised
Greatly to be praised

Father, You reign
Great are You, Lord
You're greatly to be praised

(**Great Are You Lord**, Osinachi Kalu Okoro Egbu)

Praise God from whom all blessings flow. Praise
Him all creatures here below. Praise Him above ye
Heavenly hosts. Praise Father, Son, and Holy Ghost.
(**Doxology, Praise God From Whom All Blessings
Flow**, Bishop Thomas Ken, 1674)

**To the only wise God our Saviour, *be* glory and
majesty, dominion and power both now and ever.
Amen. (Jude 1:25)**

Dear Reader

Thank you for acquiring and reading, praying and praising with this book. I hope it was simply a blessing to you and a beautiful sound from your mouth to God's ears.

Use it year-round as your praise vocabulary expands and as you grow spiritually. Praying these verses will deepen your Christian walk and your relationship with God as you go from Thanksgiving to Praise and then ascend all the way into Worship--, even into the Holy of Holies.

Get the audio book and soak in this praise.

Shalom,

Dr. Marlene Miles

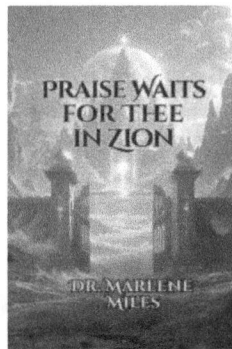

Prayerbooks by this author

While most books by this author have prayer points either throughout the book or at the end, there are some books that are only prayers. You just open up the book and pray.

Prayers Against Barrenness: *For Success in Business and Life*

Fruit of the Womb: *Prayers Against Barrenness*

Beauty Curses, *Warfare Prayers Against*
https://a.co/d/5Xlc20M

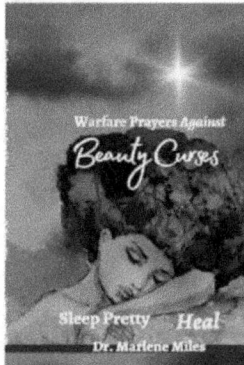

Courts of Marriage: Prayers for Marriage in the Courts of Heaven *(prayerbook)* https://a.co/d/cNAdgAq

Courtroom Warfare @ Midnight *(prayerbook)*
https://a.co/d/5fc7Qdp

Demonic Cobwebs *(prayerbook)* https://a.co/d/fp9Oa2H

Every Evil Bird https://a.co/d/hF1kh1O

Gates of Thanksgiving

Praise Waits for Thee in Zion

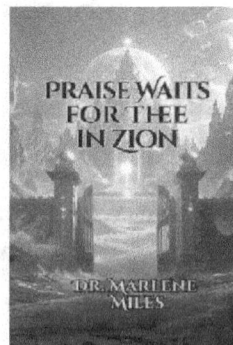

So Thankful https://a.co/d/aePABdZ

Spirits of Death, Hell & the Grave, Pass Over Me and My House

Throne of Grace: Courtroom Prayer

Warfare Prayer Against Poverty
https://a.co/d/bZ61lYu

Other books by this author

200 RED FLAGS: The Track Is Not Safe

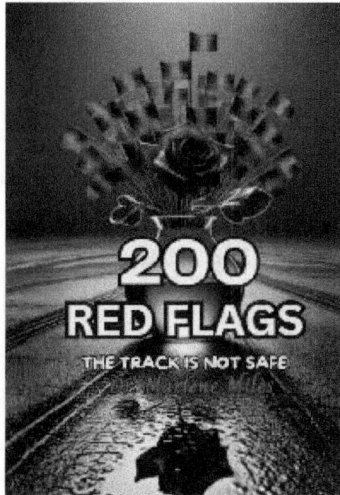

AK: The Adventures of the Agape Kid

Already Married in the Spirit: *Why You May Not Be Married in the Natural*

AMONG SOME THIEVES https://a.co/d/dkYT4ZV

Ancestral Powers

Anti-Marriage, *The Spirit of*

Backstabbers https://a.co/d/gi8iBxf

Barrenness, *Prayers Against* https://a.co/d/feUltIs

Battlefield of Marriage, *The*

Beware of the Dog: Prayers Against Dogs in the Dream.

Bless Your Food: *Let the Dining Table be Undefiled*

Blindsided: *Has the Old Man Bewitched You?*
https://a.co/d/5O2fLLR

Break Free from Collective Captivity

Broken Spirits & Dry Bones

By Means of a Whorish Father

Caged Life: Get Out Alive!

https://a.co/d/bwPbksX

Casting Down Imaginations

Churchzilla, The Wanna-Be, Supposed-to-be Bride of Christ

Demonic Cobwebs (prayerbook)

Demonic Time Bombs

Demons Hate Questions

Devil Loves Trauma, *The*

Devil Weapons: Unforgiveness, Bitterness,…

The Devourers: Thieves of Darkness 2

Do Not Swear by the Moon

Don't Refuse Me, Lord (4 book series)

https://a.co/d/idP34LG

Dream Defilement

The Emptiers: *Thieves of Darkness, 1*
https://a.co/d/5I4n5mc

Evil Touch

Failed Assignment

Fantasy Spirit Spouse https://a.co/d/hW7oYbX

FAT Demons (The): *Breaking Demonic Curses*
https://a.co/d/4kP8wV1

The Fold (5-book series)

- The Fold (Book 1)
- Name Your Seed (Book 2)
- The Poor Attitudes of Money (3)
- Do Not Orphan Your Seed (4)
- For the Sake of the Gospel (5)
- My Sowing Journal

Gang Ups: Touch Not God's Anointed

Getting Rid of Evil Spiritual Food

https://a.co/d/i2L3WYQ

got HEALING? Verses for Life

got LOVE? Verses for Life

got HOPE? Verses for Life

got money? https://a.co/d/g2av41N

Has My Soul Been Sold? https://a.co/d/dyB8hhA

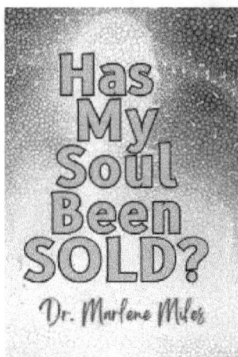

Here Come the Horns: *Skilled to Destroy*
https://a.co/d/cZiNnkP

Hidden Sins: Hidden Iniquity

https://a.co/d/4Mth0wa

How to Dental Assist

How to Dental Assist2: Be Productive, Not Wasteful

How to STOP Being a Blind Witch or Warlock

I Take It Back

Legacy

Let Me Have A Dollar's Worth
https://a.co/d/h8F8XgE

Let Them Come Up & Worship
https://a.co/d/3yEAPMW

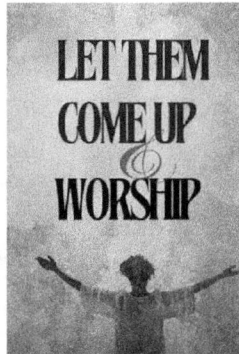

LET THEM COME UP & WORSHIP

Level the Playing Field

Living for the NOW of God

Lose My Location https://a.co/d/crD6mV9

Love Breaks Your Heart

Made Perfect In Love

Mammon https://a.co/d/29yhMG7

Man Safari, *The*

Marriage Ed. Rules of Engagement & Marriage

Made Perfect in Love

Money Hunters: Beware of Those

Money on the Altar https://a.co/d/4EqJ2Nr

Mulberry Tree, *The* https://a.co/d/9nR9rRb

Motherboard (The) - *Soul Prosperity Series*

Name Your Seed

Occupy: *Until I Return* https://a.co/d/bZ7ztUy

Opponent, Adversary, or Enemy?: Fight The Right Battle with the Right Weapons

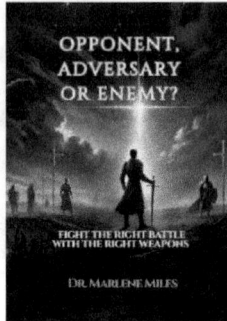

Plantation Souls

Players Gonna Play

Portals: Shut the Front Door: Prayers to Close Evil Portals.

Power Money: Nine Times the Tithe

https://a.co/d/gRt41gy

The Power to Get Wealth https://a.co/d/e4ub4Ov

Powers Above

The Robe, Part 1, The Lessons of Joseph

The Robe, Part II, The Lessons of Joseph

Seasons of Grief

Seasons of Waiting

Seasons of War

Second Marriage, Third--, *Any Marriage*

https://a.co/d/6m6GN4N

Seducing Spirits: Idolatry & Whoredoms

https://a.co/d/4Jq4WEs

Shut the Front Door: *Prayers to Close Portals*
https://a.co/d/cH4TWJj

Sift You Like Wheat

Six Men Short: What Has Happened to all the Men?

SLAVE

Sleep Afflictions & Really Bad Dreams
https://a.co/d/f8sDmgv

Soul Prosperity soul prosperity series 3

https://a.co/d/5p8YvCN

Souls Captivity soul prosperity series 2

The Spirit of Anti-Marriage

The Spirit of Poverty https://a.co/d/abV2o2e

Spiritual Thieves https://a.co/d/eqPPz33

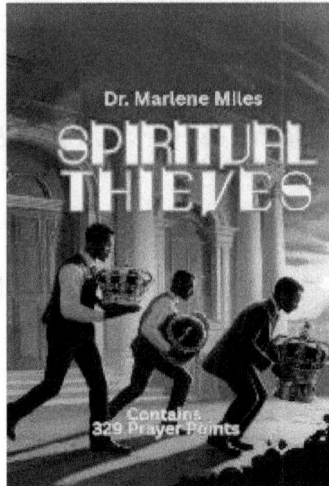

StarStruck- Triangular Power series.

SUNBLOCK- Triangular Power series.

The Swallowers: *Thieves of Darkness*, 3

Take It Back

This Is NOT That: How to Keep Demons from Coming at You

Time Is of the Essence

Too Many Wives: *Why You Have Lady Problems*

Tormenting Spirits   https://a.co/d/dAogEJf

Toxic Souls

Triangular Power *(series),* Powers Above, SUNBLOCK, Do Not Swear by the Moon, STARSTRUCK

Unbreak My Heart: *Don't Let Me Die*

Uncontested Doom

Unguarded Hours, *The*

Unseen Life, *The* (forthcoming)

Upgrade: How to Get Out of Survival Mode Toxic Souls (Book 2 of series) , Legacy (Book 3 of series)

The Wasters: *Thieves of Darkness,* Bk 2
https://a.co/d/bUvI9Jo

What Have You to Declare? What Do You Have With You from Where You've Been?

When I Was A Child, *I Prayed As a Child*

When the Devourer is Rebuked

https://a.co/d/1HVv8oq

WTH? Get Me Out of This Hell
https://a.co/d/a7WBGJh

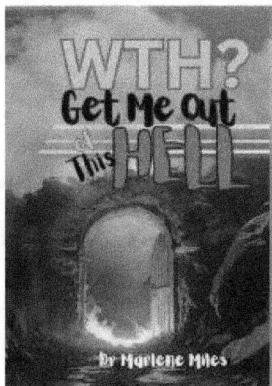

The Wilderness Romance *(series)* This series is about conducting a Godly relationship and marriage with someone who is a Wilderness person. It is about how to recognize it and navigate through it. These books are about how not to get caught up in such.

- *The Social Wilderness*
- *The Sexual Wilderness*
- *The Spiritual Wilderness*

Other Series

The Fold (a series on Godly finances)
https://a.co/d/4hz3unj

Soul Prosperity Series https://a.co/d/bz2M42q

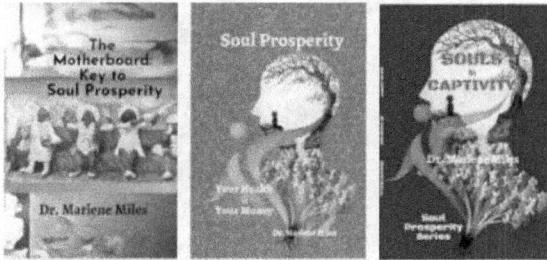

Spirit Spouse books

https://a.co/d/9VehDSo

https://a.co/d/97sKOwm

Battlefield of Marriage, The

https://a.co/d/eUDzizO

Players Gonna Play

https://a.co/d/2hzGw3N

Sent Spirit Spouse (can someone send you a spirit spouse? This book is not yet released.)

Matters of the Heart, Made Perfect in Love
https://a.co/d/70MQW3O , Love Breaks Your Heart
https://a.co/d/4KvuQLZ, Unbreak My Heart
https://a.co/d/84ceZ6M Broken Spirits & Dry Bones
https://a.co/d/e6iedNP

Thieves of Darkness series

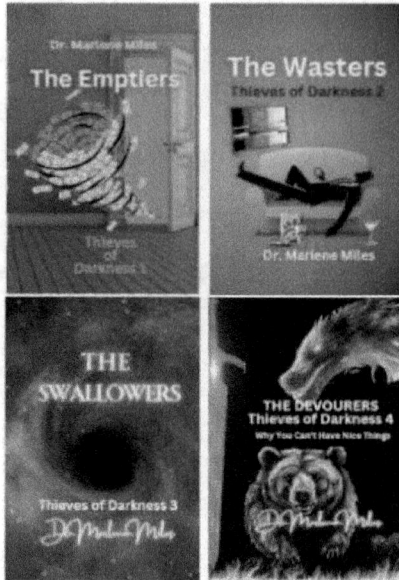

The Emptiers https://a.co/d/heio0dO

The Wasters https://a.co/d/5TG1iNQ

The Swallowers https://a.co/d/1jWhM6G

The Devourers: Why We Can't Have Nice Things
https://a.co/d/87Tejbf

Spiritual Thieves

Triangular Powers https://a.co/d/aUCjAWC

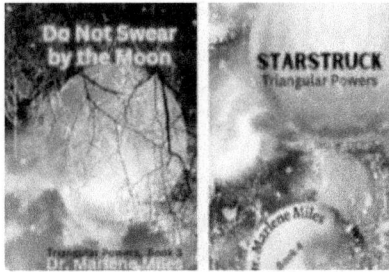

Upgrade (series) *How to Get Out of Survival Mode*
https://a.co/d/aTERhXO